RECENT POSTS AND PRAISE

One year ago my fiancé/husband decided to call it quits on me, and I was devastated. I was confused, sad, upset; you name it. Alhamdulilah though, it had led me to stumble upon your writings. This past year has been a very emotional year however an excellent learning process to mend my heart correctly. I learned only Allah belongs in the heart and the rest is a gift that belongs in the hand; even if they are halal things. Your writings have helped me so much there are no words to describe it. Three weeks ago my father Allah yirhamo (May God have mercy on him) passed away very suddenly leaving my entire family and community shocked and devastated; yet my first thought was Inna lillah w Inna elayhi raji3oon, to Allah we belong and to Him we shall return; my dad went Home inshAllah. Instead of getting upset, I found myself truly thankful Allah chose him to be my dad and let me have had him for as long as I did. Regardless of the situation, Allah always chooses the best for us, so I believe this was the best time for him to go.

I want to thank you from the bottom of my heart, because had I not learned and reflected on your writings, I don't think I would be who I am today, handling the loss of one of my favorite people in the world. I would like to say it was one specific piece of writing that inspired me, but it wasn't; it was your entire collection. I make dua Allah rewards you immensely, and continuously inspires you and allows you to keep doing what you're doing. May Allah bless and protect your loved ones. Please make dua for my father.

—Aala

I would like to extend my gratitude to you, for changing my life completely, Allah bless you dear. I was going through terrible phase of my life, darkness, depression, hollowness and negativity was all over me. Then I stumbled upon your articles. Enlightened I am now! Alhamadulillah. Thank you and keep writing as Allah "the Great" has blessed you with this quality. May Allah accept all duaa's (supplications) I'm making for you ....actually this the only one thing I can say, because no words are enough!

—Maryam I.

Your words hit me so hard I had to slow down whilst reading and breathe. I always took pride in not being superficial, in not being materialistic all the while depending on people I loved to make me happy. And when they let me down or left me, it shook my world, the very ground I stood on. There is a constant need to be loved, and from love I derive happiness. But it is a constant battle to realize that this love is to come from my relationship with

Allah and not people. I'm an idealist, a giver, giving joy to others makes me happy; but it is so hard to understand and remember that no, these people, this life, is not to be expected of. Alhumdulillah reading your words was like taking a good hard look at myself, one that I wasn't ready to take… this helps so much. God bless you for being real.

—Mehar

I just want to take this time to tell you that I absolutely love your articles. I am an avid reader since I was 8. I have devoured the self-help sections in book stores, I love Rumi, Ghazzali, Iqbal, and many many amazing writers who speak to the soul. Why am I telling you this- because after reading the writings of so many brilliant people, I have found my heart and soul in your work. You are definitely one of my favorite writers. Whenever I need inspiration I go back to your articles. Also I have found someone I love dearly, I consider him my soul mate, and my love for him has made me so attached to him. It is only through your work that I am learning to love the One who is never lost and holding on to the Bond that never breaks! You have taught me what true love is really about! I love your work. You inspire me immensely. And yes my brother too loves your work, so do my friends. I pray that Allah gives you everything of the best and continues making you a means to inspire us all towards His love! With much love, hugs and duas!

—Mohsina, South Africa

I chanced upon your website and videos not too long ago. Just before that I've been seeking out 'food for my soul' for my heart. Words that would heal my rusty heart. Then I came across your blog and videos. Mashallah, sister I have no words to describe the effect your writings have on my heart and soul. Each word you write touches my heart and crumbles my nafs (ego) and brings me to tears. I cannot thank you enough for your inspirational work and for the constant reminders that you give us through your work. May Allah (swt) grant you the highest Jannah and reward you in dunya and aakhira.
Thank you thank you and thank you.

—Muneera, Singapore

Tawakkul Karman reminds me of Yasmin Mogahed. The former sparks an outer revolution and the latter sparks an internal revolution.

—mA

Yasmin, I don't know you and you don't know me, but I feel that you're so close to me! Every single would you wrote touches me deeply!

—Noor

I think I was living a hypocritical life, where I just say that I love Allah, but my actions do not reflect the same. The Transformation in my life came when I started knowing the real essence and meaning of LOVE Allah from your articles and lectures. Alhamdulillah. And soon then EVERYTHING in my life set STRAIGHT..!

—Nazeer

MashAllah, Allah has gifted you with the ability to penetrate right to one's heart, shake it and get it to start working the way it should! Thank You Allah for people like Yasmin Mogahed :)

—Ghazi A.

May Allah bless you and protect you forever and ever. May you go to heaven and live there happily ever after. Never under estimate the lives your words touch. Inshallahrabanayanthur 3aleiki be3ayn al rida tonight (May God look at you with the eye of contentment tonight)! If there was a place deeper than the heart then it would have been from there. I just truly wanted you to know what an amazing gift and inspiration you have been to the Muslim society-in particular the youth. You may or may not realize it, but so many of your points really hit home with all of the problems we are dealing with in this world.

In this current world where everything seems to be going downhill, you represent more than just a "good writer" or a "good lecturer"; you represent hope! Hope that there are still genuine and pure people out there. Also you may not know this but what people often say about you is that there is something ever so comforting about your presence and not something one can put their finger on. I personally put this down to truth. When someone speaks such true words in your presence the heart cannot help but react.

You have helped many people make it through the darkest of times and for that may Allah reward you. You have gotten a lot of people to do good deeds which they wouldn't have done before and for that may Allah reward you. Inshallah your hasanat (good deeds) keep rolling over like the millionaire's dollars keep rolling. But the difference is on the day of Judgment. Inshallah you will be a billion times wealthier then they are and I hope to bear witness to that. I hope you are welcomed by the Prophet Muhammed صلى الله عليه وسلم with the biggest of smiles and warmest of hugs as you are one of his followers who have genuinely tried to make a difference in this world and you HAVE made a difference.

I'm sorry if this seems slightly exaggerated but in your writing I found strength to hold onto Allah at my weakest. I only wish I grew up around you as I could do with a friend with strong iman. This is on behalf of thousands of people inspired by you all the way here in London.

Jazak Allah Alf Alfkheir inshallah.

I think I should stop now or I will go on forever. Salam Aleikum.

—Mohamed A.

I am reading this article after a year and thinking that THIS is the article that in fact changed me. I was never really into Islam nor was I practicing that much. My life was in darkness, with people who only brought me down to a person who wasn't meant to be. So I fell deep into the dunya. I did things that I am not proud of, at all. I kept failing and failing and falling and falling. I was stumbling and I didn't know myself anymore until one night something terrible happened and I knew at that moment that Allah was in fact always there but it was me, who was ignoring Him. Ignoring the creator. That night, I told myself that enough was enough and I came back into Islam. I came back to Him. After that night, I went on a journey to change my life. That journey, with Allah being my captain, I was able to turn my life 360. Today, I don't remember my life without the hijab. Today, I don't remember my life without praying or going daily to the Masjid or going to my daily halaqas. Yasmin, I cannot thank you enough for posting this article and really getting deep into everyone's hearts. I listened to what you said; I took the keys from the dunya and gave them to the Creator. You are such an inspiring woman and I look up to you :) Thank you so so much.

—Humaira

May Allah (swt) reward you with Firdous (the highest heaven). Ameen. I cannot even express what a blessing you are sister Yasmin. Your coming into my life through your writing strengthens my emaan (faith) day by day alhamdulillah (all praise is due to God) and inspires so many of my friends and loved ones with whom I often share your work with! Allah swt has truly answered your dua if you prayed to be used as a tool to guide the ummah! :)

—Hajera M.

Reclaim Your Heart

Personal Insights on Breaking Free
From Life's Shackles

Yasmin Mogahed

FB PUBLISHING

SAN CLEMENTE

Published in the United States of America

FB Publishing
645 Camino De Los Mares
Suite 108-276
San Clemente, CA 92673
Visit our website at www.fbpublishinghouse.com

9 8 7 6 5 4 3 2 1

Internal Photographs: SignsOfTheDivine.com
Book Design: Daniel Middleton | www.scribefreelance.com

Library of Congress Cataloging-in-Publication Data

Mogahed, Yasmin.
   Reclaim your heart: personal insights on breaking free from life's shackles / Yasmin Mogahed.
p. cm.
   1. Spirituality. 2. Religion. 3. Inspiration. 4. Self Help. I. Title.

ISBN
978-0-9857512-0-3

Printed in the United States of America
First Printing August 2012

DEDICATION

"This book is dedicated, in its entirety, to the One who has raised me even before I was in my mother's womb. It is dedicated to the One who has taught me, inspired me and guided me throughout my life. I dedicate this humble endeavor to God, and I only pray that in spite of my weakness, it may be accepted, and to my family who has supported me throughout the journey."

INTRODUCTION

Reclaim Your Heart is not just a self-help book. It is a manual about the journey of the heart in and out of the ocean of this life. It is a book about how to keep your heart from sinking to the depths of that ocean, and what to do when it does. It is a book about redemption, about hope, about renewal. Every heart can heal, and each moment is created to bring us closer to that transformative return. *Reclaim Your Heart* is about finding that moment when everything stops and suddenly looks different. It is about finding your own awakening. And then returning to the better, truer, and freer version of yourself.

Contents

ATTACHMENTS

WHY DO PEOPLE HAVE TO LEAVE EACH OTHER?

When I was 17 years old, I had a dream. I dreamt that I was sitting inside a masjid and a little girl walked up to ask me a question. She asked me, "Why do people have to leave each other?" The question was a personal one, but it seemed clear to me why the question was chosen for me.

I was one to get attached.

Ever since I was a child, this temperament was clear. While other children in preschool could easily recover once their parents left, I could not. My tears, once set in motion, did not stop easily. As I grew up, I learned to become attached to everything around me. From the time I was in first grade, I needed a best friend. As I got older, any fall-out with a friend shattered me. I couldn't let go of anything. People, places, events, photographs, moments—even outcomes became objects of strong attachment. If things didn't work out the way I wanted or imagined they should, I was devastated. And disappointment for me wasn't an ordinary emotion. It was catastrophic. Once let down, I never fully recovered. I could never forget, and the break never mended. Like a glass vase that you place on the edge of a table, once broken, the pieces never quite fit again.

However the problem wasn't with the vase, or even that the vases kept breaking. The problem was that I kept putting them on the edge of tables. Through my attachments, I was dependent on my relationships to fulfill my needs. I allowed those relationships to define my happiness or my sadness, my fulfillment or my emptiness, my security, and even my self-worth. And so, like the vase placed where it will inevitably fall, through those dependencies I set myself up for disappointment. I set myself up to be broken. And that's exactly what I found: one disappointment, one break after another.

Yet the people who broke me were not to blame any more than gravity can be blamed for breaking the vase. We can't blame the laws of physics when a twig snaps because we leaned on it for support. The twig was never created to carry us.

Our weight was only meant to be carried by God. We are told in the Quran: "...whoever rejects evil and believes in God hath grasped the most trustworthy hand-hold that never breaks. And God hears and knows all things." (Qur'an, 2: 256)

There is a crucial lesson in this verse: that there is only one hand-hold that never breaks. There is only one place where we can lay our dependencies. There is only one relationship that should define our self-worth and only one source from which to seek our ultimate happiness, fulfillment, and security. That place is God.

However, this world is all about seeking those things everywhere else. Some of us seek it in our careers; some seek it in wealth, some in status. Some, like me, seek it in our relationships. In her book, Eat, Pray, Love, Elizabeth Gilbert describes her own quest for happiness. She describes moving in and out of relationships, and even traveling the globe in search of this fulfillment. She seeks that fulfillment--unsuccessfully--in her relationships, in meditation, even in food.

And that's exactly where I spent much of my own life: seeking a way to fill my inner void. So it was no wonder that the little girl in my dream asked me this question. It was a question about loss, about disappointment. It was a question about being let down. A question about seeking something and coming back empty handed. It was about what happens when you try to dig in concrete with your bare hands: not only do you come back with nothing—you break your fingers in the process. I learned this not by reading it, not by hearing it from a wise sage, I learned it by trying it again, and again, and again.

And so, the little girl's question was essentially my own question…being asked to myself.

Ultimately, the question was about the nature of the dunya as a place of fleeting moments and temporary attachments. As a place where people are with you today and leave or die tomorrow. But this reality hurts our very being because it goes against our nature. We, as humans, are made to seek, love, and strive for what is perfect and what is permanent. We are made to seek what's eternal. We seek this because we were not made for this life. Our first and true home was Paradise: a land that is both perfect and eternal. So the yearning for that type of life is a part of our being. The problem is that we try to find that here. And so we create ageless creams and cosmetic surgery in a desperate attempt to hold on—in an attempt to mold this world into what it is not, and will never be.

And that's why if we live in dunya with our hearts, it breaks us. That's why this dunya hurts. It is because the definition of dunya, as something temporary and imperfect, goes against everything we are made to yearn for. Allah put a yearning in us that can only be fulfilled by what is eternal and perfect. By trying to find fulfillment in what is fleeting, we are running after a hologram…a mirage. We are digging into concrete with our bare hands. Seeking to turn, what is by its very nature temporary into something eternal is like trying to extract from fire, water. You just get burned. Only when we stop putting our hopes in dunya, only when we stop trying to make the dunya into what it is not—and was never meant to be (jannah)—will this life finally stop breaking our hearts.

We must also realize that nothing happens without a purpose. Nothing. Not even broken hearts. Not even pain. That broken heart and that pain are lessons and signs for us. They are warnings that something is wrong. They are warnings that we need to make a change. Just like the pain of being burned is what warns us to remove our hand from the fire, emotional pain warns us that we need to make an internal change. We need to detach. Pain is a form of forced detachment. Like the loved one who hurts you again and again and again, the more dunya hurts us, the more we inevitably detach from it. The more we inevitably stop loving it.

And pain is a pointer to our attachments. That which makes us cry, that which causes us the most pain is where our false attachments lie. And it is those things which we are attached to as we should only be attached to Allah which become barriers on our path to God. But the pain itself is what makes the false attachment evident. The pain creates a condition in our life that we seek to change, and if there is anything about our condition that we don't like, there is a divine formula to change it. God says: "Verily never will God change the condition of a people until they change what is within themselves." (Qur'an, 13:11)

After years of falling into the same pattern of disappointments and heartbreak, I finally began to realize something profound. I had always thought that love of dunya meant being attached to material things. And I was not attached to material things. I was attached to people. I was attached to moments. I was attached to emotions. So I thought that the love of dunya just did not apply to me. What I didn't realize was that people, moments, emotions are all a part of dunya. What I didn't realize is that all the pain I had experienced in life was due to one thing and one thing only: love of dunya.

As soon as I began to have that realization, a veil was lifted from my eyes. I started to see what my problem was. I was expecting this life to be what it is not, and was never meant to be: perfect. And being the idealist that I am, I was struggling with every cell in my body to make it so. It had to be perfect.

And I would not stop until it was. I gave my blood, sweat, and tears to this endeavor: making the dunya into jannah. This meant expecting people around me to be perfect. Expecting my relationships to be perfect. Expecting so much from those around me and from this life. Expectations. Expectations. Expectations. And if there is one recipe for unhappiness it is that: expectations. But herein lay my fatal mistake. My mistake was not in having expectations; as humans, we should never lose hope. The problem was in *where* I was placing those expectations and that hope. At the end of the day, my hope and expectations were not being placed in God. My hope and expectations were in people, relationships, means. Ultimately, my hope was in this dunya rather than Allah.

And so I came to realize a very deep Truth. An ayah began to cross my mind. It was an ayah I had heard before, but for the first time I realized that it was actually describing me: "Those who rest not their hope on their meeting with Us, but are pleased and satisfied with the life of the present, and those who heed not Our Signs." (Qur'an, 10:7)

By thinking that I can have everything here, my hope was not in my meeting with God. My hope was in dunya. But what does it mean to place your hope in dunya? How can this be avoided? It means when you have friends, don't expect your friends to fill your emptiness. When you get married, don't expect your spouse to fulfill your every need. When you're an activist, don't put your hope in the results. When you're in trouble don't depend on yourself. Don't depend on people. Depend on God.

Seek the help of people—but realize that it is not the people (or even your own self) that can save you. Only Allah can do these things. The people are only tools, a means used by God. But they are not the source of help, aid, or salvation of any kind. Only God is. The people cannot even create the wing of a fly (Quran, 22:73). And so, even while you interact with people externally, turn your heart towards God. Face Him alone, as Prophet Ibrahim (as) said so beautifully: "For me, I have set my face, firmly and truly, towards Him Who created the heavens and the earth, and never shall I give partners to Allah." (Qur'an, 6:79)

But how does Prophet Ibrahim (as) describe his journey to that point? He studies the moon, the sun and the stars and realizes that they are not perfect. They set.

They let us down.

So Prophet Ibrahim (as) was thereby led to face Allah alone. Like him, we need to put our full hope, trust, and dependency on God, and God alone. And if we do that, we will learn what it means to finally find peace and stability of heart. Only then will the roller coaster that once defined our lives finally come to an end. That is because if our inner state is dependent on something that is by definition inconstant, that inner state will also be inconstant. If our inner state is dependent on something changing and temporary, that inner state will be in a constant state of instability, agitation, and unrest. This means that one moment we're happy, but as soon as that which our happiness depended upon changes, our happiness also changes. And we become sad. We remain always swinging from one extreme to another and not realizing why.

We experience this emotional roller coaster because we can never find stability and lasting peace until our attachment and dependency is on what is stable and lasting. How can we hope to find constancy if what we hold on to is inconstant and perishing? In the statement of Abu Bakr is a deep illustration of this truth. After the Prophet Muhammad ﷺ died, the people went into shock and could not handle the news. Although no one loved the Prophet ﷺ like Abu Bakr, Abu Bakr understood well the only place where one's dependency should lie. He said: "If you worshipped Muhammad, know that Muhammad is dead. But if you worshipped Allah, know that Allah never dies."

To attain that state, don't let your source of fulfillment be anything other than your relationship with God. Don't let your definition of success, failure, or self-worth be anything other than your position with Him (Qur'an, 49:13). And if you do this, you become unbreakable, because your hand-hold is unbreakable. You become unconquerable, because your supporter can never be conquered. And you will never become empty, because your source of fulfillment is unending and never diminishes.

Looking back at the dream I had when I was 17, I wonder if that little girl was me. I wonder this because the answer I gave her was a lesson, I would need to spend the next painful years of my life learning. My answer to her question of why people have to leave each other was: "because this life isn't perfect; for if it was, what would the next be called?"

PEOPLE LEAVE, BUT DO THEY RETURN?

Leaving is hard. Losing is harder. So a few weeks ago I asked the question, 'why do people have to leave each other?' The answer took me into some of my life's deepest realizations and struggles. However, it has also led me to wonder: After people leave, do they ever return? After something we love is taken from us, does it ever come back? Is loss permanent—or just a means for a higher purpose? Is loss the End itself, or a temporary cure for our heart's ailments?

There's something amazing about this life. The very same worldly attribute that causes us pain is also what gives us relief: Nothing here lasts. What does that mean? It means that the breathtakingly beautiful rose in my vase will wither tomorrow. It means that my youth will neglect me. But it also means that the sadness I feel today will change tomorrow. My pain will die. My laughter won't last forever—but neither will my tears. We say this life isn't perfect. And it isn't. It isn't perfectly good. But, it also isn't perfectly bad, either.

Allah (glorified is He) tells us in a very profound ayah (verse): "Verily with hardship comes ease." (Qur'an, 94:5). Growing up I think I understood this ayah wrongly. I used to think it meant: after hardship comes ease. In other words, I thought life was made up of good times and bad times. After the bad times, come the good times. I thought this as if life was either all good or all bad. But that is not what the ayah is saying. The ayah is saying WITH hardship comes ease. The ease is at the same time as the hardship. This means that nothing in this life is ever all bad (or all good). In every bad situation we're in, there is always something to be grateful for. With hardship, Allah also gives us the strength and patience to bear it.

If we study the difficult times in our lives, we will see that they were also filled with much good. The question is—which do we chose to focus on? I think the trap we fall into is rooted in this false belief that this life can be perfect—perfectly good or perfectly bad. However that's not the nature of dunya (this life). That's the nature of the hereafter. The hereafter is saved for the perfection of things. Jannah (paradise) is perfectly and completely good. There is no bad in it. And Jahannam (hell—may Allah protect us) is perfectly and completely bad. There is no good in it.

By not truly understanding this reality, I myself would become consumed by the momentary circumstances of my life (whether good or bad). I experienced each situation in its full intensity—as if it was ultimate or would never end. The way I was feeling at the moment transformed the whole world and everything in it. If I was happy in that moment, past and present, near and far, the entire universe was good for that moment. As if perfection could exist here. And the same happened with bad things. A negative state consumed everything. It became the whole world, past and present, the entire universe was bad for that moment. Because it became my entire universe, I could see nothing outside of it. Nothing else existed for that moment. If you wronged me today, it was because you no longer cared about me—not because this was one moment of a string of infinite moments which happened to be tinted that way, or because you and I and this life just aren't perfect. What I was experiencing or feelings at that instant replaced context, because it replaced my entire vision of the world.

I think in our experiential nature, some of us maybe especially susceptible to this. Perhaps that is the reason we can fall prey to the "I've never seen good from you" phenomenon which the Prophet ﷺ (peace be upon him) referred to in his hadith. Perhaps some of us say or feel this way because at that moment, experientially we really haven't seen good, because our feeling at that instant replaces, defines and becomes everything. Past and present becomes rolled up into one experiential moment.

But, the true realization that nothing is complete in this life transforms our experience of it. We suddenly stop being consumed by moments. In the understanding that nothing is limitless here, that nothing here is kamil (perfect, complete), Allah enables us to step outside of moments and see them for what they are: not universes, not reality, past and present, just that—a single moment in a string of infinite moments…and that they too shall pass.

When I cry or lose or bruise, so long as I am still alive, nothing is ultimate. So long as there is still a tomorrow, a next moment, there is hope, there is change, and there is redemption. What is lost is not lost forever.

So in answering the question of whether what is lost comes back, I study the most beautiful examples. Did Yusuf return to his father? Did Musa return to his mother? Did Hajar return to Ibrahim? Did health, wealth and children return to Ayoub? From these stories we learn a powerful and beautiful lesson: what is taken by Allah is never lost. In fact, it is only what is with Allah that remains. Everything else vanishes. Allah (swt) says, "What is with you must vanish: what is with Allah will endure. And We will certainly bestow, on those who patiently persevere, their reward according to the best of their actions." (Quran, 16:96)

So, all that is with Allah, is never lost. In fact the Prophet ﷺ has said: "You will never give up a thing for the sake of Allah (swt), but that Allah will replace it for you with something that is better for you than it." (Ahmad) Did not Allah take the husband of Umm Salamah, only to replace him with the Prophet ﷺ?

Sometimes Allah takes in order to give. But, it's crucial to understand that His giving is not always in the form we think we want. He knows best what is best. Allah says: "… But it is possible that you dislike a thing which is good for you, and that you love a thing which is bad for you. But Allah knows, and you know not." (Quran, 2:216)

But if something is going to be returned in one form or another, why is it taken at all? Subhan'Allah. It is in the process of 'losing' that we are given.

Allah gives us gifts, but then we often become dependent on those gifts, instead of Him. When He gives us money, we depend on the money—not Him. When He gives us people, we depend on people—not Him. When He gives us status or power, we depend on, and become distracted by these things. When Allah gives us health, we become deceived. We think we will never die.

Allah gives us gifts, but then we come to love them as we should only love Him. We take those gifts and inject them into our hearts, until they take over. Soon we cannot live without them. Every waking moment is spent in contemplation of them, in submission and worship to them. The mind and the heart that was created by Allah, for Allah, becomes the property of someone or something else. And then the fear comes, the fear of loss begins to cripple us. The gift—that should have remained in our hands—takes over our heart, so the fear of losing it consumes us. Soon, what was once a gift becomes a weapon of torture and a prison of our own making. How can we be freed of this? At times, in His infinite mercy, Allah frees us…by taking it away.

As a result of it being taken, we turn to Allah wholeheartedly. In that desperation and need, we ask, we beg, we pray. Through the loss, we reach a level of sincerity and humility and dependence on Him which we would otherwise not reach—had it not been taken from us. Through the loss, our hearts turn entirely to face Him.

What happens when you first give a child a toy or the new video game he's always wanted? He becomes consumed by it. Soon he wants to do nothing else. He sees nothing else. He doesn't want to do his work or even eat. He's hypnotized to his own detriment. So what do you do, as a loving parent? Do you leave him to drown in his addiction and complete loss of focus and balance? No.

You take it away.

Then, once the child has regained focus of his priorities, regained sanity and balance, once things are put in their proper place in his heart and mind and life, what happens? You give the gift back. Or perhaps something better. But this time, the gift is no longer in his heart. It is in its proper place. It is in his hand.

Yet in that process of taking, the most important thing happened. The losing and regaining of the gift is inconsequential. The taking of your heedlessness, your dependence and focus on other than Him, and the replacing it with remembrance, dependence and focus only on Him was the real gift. Allah withholds to give.

And so sometimes, the 'something better' is the greatest gift: nearness to Him. Allah took the daughter of Malik Ibn Dinar in order to save him. He took his daughter, but replaced her with protection from the hell-fire and salvation from a painful life of sin and distance from Him. Through the loss of his daughter, Malik ibn Dinar was blessed with a life spent in nearness to Allah. And even that which was taken (his daughter) would remain with Malik ibn Dinar forever in Jannah.

Ibn ul Qayyim (may Allah be pleased with him) speaks about this phenomenon in his book, Madarij Al Salikin. He says: "The divine decree related to the believer is always a bounty, even if it is in the form of withholding (something that is desired); and it is a blessing, even if it appears to be a trial and an affliction that has befallen him; it is in reality a cure, even though it appears to be a disease!"

So to the question, 'once something is lost, does it return?' the answer is, yes. It returns. Sometimes here, sometime there, sometimes in a different, better form. But the greatest gift lies beneath the taking and the returning. Allah tells tells us: "Say, 'In the bounty of Allah and in His mercy—in that let them rejoice; it is better than what they hoard.'" (Quran, 10:58)

ON FILLING THE INNER HOLE AND COMING HOME

We're Home.

And then we aren't. Torn away from our origin, we came across time and space to another world. A lesser world. But in that separation, something painful happened. We were no longer with God in the physical space. We could no longer see Him with our physical eyes, or speak to Him with our physical voice. Unlike our father Adam (`alayhi as-salam—peace be upon him), we could no longer feel that same peace.

So we came down. We were torn from Him. And in the pain of that separation, we bled. For the first time, we bled. And that tearing apart from our Creator left a gash. A deep wound that we are all born with. And as we grew, so did the agony of that wound; it grew deeper and deeper. But as time went on, we moved further and further away from the antidote, already in our fitrah (nature): to be near Him, heart, soul and mind.

And so with each passing year, we became more and more desperate to fill that empty space. But it is in this very quest to fill the hole that we stumbled. Each of us stumbled on different things. And many of us sought to numb the emptiness. So, some of humanity stumbled on drugs or alcohol, while some looked to other sedatives. Some of us stumbled on the worship of physical pleasure, status or money. Some of us lost ourselves in our careers.

And then, some of us stumbled on people. Some of us lost ourselves there.

But, what if every single stumble, every challenge, every experience in our life was only intended for one purpose: to bring us back to our origin? What if every win, every loss, every beauty, every fall, every cruelty, and every smile was only intended to unveil another barrier between us and God? Between us and where we began, and where we are desperately seeking to return?

What if everything was only about seeing Him?

We must know that all that we experience in life has a purpose. And it is we who choose whether to realize that purpose or not. Take for example, beauty. Some people don't even recognize beauty when it's right in front of them. They can walk through a sunset or a brilliant forest of orange trees, and not even notice.

Other people see beauty and do appreciate it. They will stop and take it in. They may even feel overwhelmed by it. But it ends there. That person is like the one who appreciates art, but never inquires about the artist. The artwork itself was intended to communicate a message from the artist; but if the art lover loses himself in the painting—but never sees the message, that artwork hasn't fulfilled its true purpose.

The purpose of the glorious sun, first fallen snow, crescent moons and breathtaking oceans is not just to decorate this lonely planet. The purpose is far deeper than that. The purpose is as Allah told us in the Qur'an:

إن في خلق السماوات والأرض واختلاف الليل والنهار لآيات لأولي الألباب

"Indeed, in the creation of the heavens and the earth and the alternation of the night and the day are signs for those of understanding."

الذين يذكرون الله قياما وقعودا وعلى جنوبهم ويتفكرون في خلق السماوات

والأرض ربنا ما خلقت هذا باطلا سبحانك فقنا عذاب النار

"(Those) who remember Allah while standing or sitting or [lying] on their sides and give thought to the creation of the heavens and the earth, [saying], "Our Lord, You have not created all of this without a purpose. Exalted is You [above such a thing]; then protect us from the punishment of the Fire." (Qur'an, 3:190-191)

All this beauty was created as a sign—but one that can only be understood by a select group: those who reflect (think, understand, use their intellect) and remember God in every human condition (standing, sitting, lying down).

So, even the sunset must be looked through. Even there, we cannot lose ourselves. We must look beyond even that majestic beauty and color, to see the Beauty behind it. For the beauty behind it is the True beauty, the Source of all beauty. All that we see is only a reflection.

We must study the stars, the trees, the snow-capped mountains in order to read the message behind them. Because if we do not, we are like the one who finds a message inside a beautifully decorated bottle, yet becomes so enamored by the bottle, that he never even opens the message.

But what is that message, stuck inside the intensity of stars? There is a sign— but a sign of what? These signs are a pointer to Him, to His greatness, His majesty, His beauty. A pointer to His might and His power. Study, reflect, absorb the beauty and majesty of what's created—but don't stop there. Don't lose yourself in beauty. Look beyond it and consider that if the creation is that majestic, that great, that beautiful, how majestic and great and beautiful must be the Creator.

Finally realize, experientially, that: رَبَّنَا مَا خَلَقْتَ هَذَا بَاطِلًا سُبْحَانَكَ - "My Lord, You have not created all of this without a purpose. Exalted is You." (Qur'an, 3:191)

Purpose, everything has one. Nothing in the heavens or the earth or inside of me or inside of you is created without a purpose. No event in your life, no sadness, no delight, no pain, no pleasure… no loss, was created without a purpose. So just as we must read the 'message inside the bottle' of the sun and the moon and the sky, so too must we examine the messages in our own life experiences.

We are always looking for signs. We are always asking for God to 'speak' to us. But those signs are all around us. They are in everything. God is always 'speaking'. The question is whether we are listening.

Allah says:

وقال الذين لا يعلمون لولا يكلمنا الله أو تأتينا آية كذلك قال الذين من قبلهم مثل قولهم تشابهت قلوبهم قد بينا الآيات لقوم يوقنون

"Those who do not know say, 'Why does Allah not speak to us or there come to us a sign?' Thus spoke those before them like their words. Their hearts resemble each other. We have shown clearly the signs to a people who are certain [in faith]." (Qur'an, 2:118)

If we can look beyond and through everything that happens to us, everything we do—or fail to do—and see Allah, then we will have gotten the purpose. When something happens that you love, be careful not to miss the point. Remember that nothing happens without a reason. Seek it out. Look for the purpose Allah created in what He has given to you. What aspect of His Essence is He showing you through it? What does He want from you?

Similarly, when something happens that you dislike, or that hurts you, be careful not to get lost in the illusion created by pain. Look through it. Find the message in the bottle. Find the purpose. And let it lead you to glimpse just a little more of Him.

If it's a slip or even a fall in your deen (religion), don't let shaytan (satan) deceive you. Let the slip make you witness His mercy in a more experiential and deep way. And then seek that mercy to save you from your sins and your own transgression against yourself.

If it's an unsolvable problem, don't despair. Witness a glimpse of Al-Fataah, the One who opens for His slaves any closed matter. And if it is a storm, don't let yourself drown. Let it bring you to witness how only He can save His servant from a storm, when there is no one else around.

And remember that after all of creation is destroyed and not a single being exists but Him, God will ask: لِّمَنِ الْمُلْكُ الْيَوْمَ - "To whom is the dominion today?" (Qur'an, 40:16)

Allah says:

يوم هم بارزون لا يَخفى على الله منهم شيء لمن الملك اليوم لله الواحد القهار

"The Day they come forth nothing concerning them will be concealed from Allah. To whom belongs [all] sovereignty this Day? To Allah, the One, the Irresistible!" (Qur'an, 40:16)

To whom is the sovereignty today? Try to witness even a piece of that in this life. To whom is the dominion today? Who else has the power to save you? Who else can cure you? Who else can mend your heart? Who else can provide for you? Who else can you run to? Who else? To whom is the dominion today? Li man al mulk al yawm?

Lil Wahid al Qahaar. To the One, the Irresistible. To run to anything else is to resist the irresistible. To seek other than The One (al Wahid), is to become scattered, but never filled. How can we find unity, completion of heart or soul or mind in anything other than Him?

So, on this path back to where we began, who else can we run to? What else can we seek? After all, we all want the very same thing: To be whole, to be happy, to again say:

We're Home.

EMPTYING THE VESSEL

Before you can fill any vessel, you must first empty it. The heart is a vessel. And like any vessel, the heart too must be emptied—before it can be filled. One can never hope to fill the heart with God, so long as that vessel is full of other than Him *subhanahu wa ta'ala* (exalted is He).

To empty the heart does not mean to not love. On the contrary, true love, as God intended it, is purest when it is not based on a false attachment. The process of first emptying the heart can be found in the beginning half of the *shahada* (declaration of faith). Notice that the declaration of faith begins with a critical negation, a crucial emptying. Before we hope to reach true *tawheed* (true monotheism), before we can assert our belief in the one Lord, we first assert: "*la illaha*" (there is no *illah*). An *illah* is an object of worship. But it is imperative to understand that an *illah* is not just something we pray to. An *illah* is what we revolve our life around, what we obey and what is of utmost importance to us—above all else.

It is something that we live for—and cannot live without.

So every person—atheist, agnostic, Muslim, Christian, Jew—has an *illah*. Everyone worships something. For most people, that object of worship is something from this worldly life, *dunya*. Some people worship wealth, some worship status, some worship fame, some worship their own intellect. Some people worship other people. And many, as the Qur'an describes, worship their own selves, their own desires and whims. Allah (swt) says:

أفرأيت من اتخذ إلهه هواه وأضله الله على علم وختم على سمعه وقلبه وجعل على بصره غشاوة فمن يهديه من بعد الله أفلا تذكرون

"Have you seen he who has taken as his god his [own] desire? Allah has, knowing (him as such), left him astray, and sealed his hearing and his heart (and understanding), and put a cover on his sight. Who, then, will guide him after Allah (has withdrawn Guidance)? Will you not then receive admonition?" (Qur'an, 45:23)

These objects of worship are things to which we become attached. However an object of attachment is not just something that we love. It is something that we *need*, in the deepest sense of the word. It is something that if lost, causes absolute devastation. If there is anything—or anyone—other than God that we could never give up, then we have a false attachment. Why was Prophet Ibrahim (as) told to sacrifice his son? It was to free him. It was to free him from a false attachment. Once he was free, his object of love (not attachment) was given back to him.

If there is anything—or anyone—that losing would absolutely break us, we have a false attachment. False attachments are things that we fear losing almost to a pathological extent. It is something that if we even *sense* is drifting away, we will desperately pursue. We chase it because losing an object of attachment causes complete devastation, and the severity of that devastation is proportional to the degree of attachment. These attachments can be to money, our belongings, other people, an idea, physical pleasure, a drug, status symbols, our careers, our image, how others view us, our physical appearance or beauty, the way we dress or appear to others, our degrees, our job titles, our sense of control, or our own intelligence and rationality. But until we can break these false attachments, we cannot empty the vessel of our heart. And if we do not empty that vessel, we cannot truly fill it with Allah.

This struggle to free one's heart from all false attachments, the struggle to empty the vessel of the heart, is the greatest struggle of earthly life. That struggle is the essence of *tawheed* (true monotheism). And so you will see that, if examined deeply, all five pillars of Islam are essentially about and enable detachment:

Shahada (Declaration of faith): The declaration of faith is the verbal profession of the very detachment we seek to achieve: that the only object of our worship, ultimate devotion, love, fears, and hope is God. And God alone. To succeed at freeing oneself from all other attachments, except the attachment to the Creator, is the truest manifestation of *tawheed*.

Salah (5 Daily Prayers): Five times a day we must pull away from the dunya to focus on our Creator and ultimate purpose. Five times a day, we detach ourselves from whatever we are doing of worldly life, and turn to God. Prayer could have been prescribed only once a day or week or all five prayers could have been done at one time each day, but it is not. The prayers are spread throughout the day. If one keeps to their prayers at their specified times, there is no opportunity to get attached. As soon as we begin to become engrossed in whatever dunya matter we're involved in (the job we're doing, the show we're watching, the test we're studying for, the person we can't get off our mind), we are forced to detach from it and turn our focus to the only true object of attachment.

Siyam (Fasting): Fasting is all about detachment. It is the detachment from food, drink, sexual intimacy, vain speech. By restraining our physical self, we ennoble, purify, and exalt our spiritual self. Through fasting we are forced to detach ourselves from our physical needs, desires, and pleasures.

Zakat (Charity): Zakat is about detaching ourselves from our money and giving it for the sake of God. By giving it away, we are forced to break our attachment to wealth.

Hajj (Pilgrimage): Hajj is one of the most comprehensive and profound acts of detachment. A pilgrim leaves behind everything in his life. He gives up his family, his home, his six figure salary, his warm bed, his comfortable shoes and brand name clothes, all in exchange for sleeping on the ground or in a crowded tent and wearing only two simple pieces of cloth. There are no status symbols at Hajj. No Tommy Hilfiger ihram, no five star tents. (Hajj packages that advertise 5 star hotels, are talking about before or after the Hajj. During Hajj you sleep in a tent in Mena, and on the ground, under only sky, in Muzdalifah).

Realize that God, in His infinite wisdom and mercy, does not just ask us to be detached from the *dunya*—He tells us exactly how. Beyond the five pillars, even our dress breeds detachment. The Prophet ﷺ tells us to distinguish ourselves, to be different from the crowd, even in how we appear. By wearing your *hijab*, *kufi* or beard, you can't just blend in—even if you wanted to. The Prophet ﷺ said: "Islam began as something strange, and it shall return to being something strange as it began, so give glad tidings to the strangers." [Sahih Muslim]

By being 'strange' to this *dunya*, we can live in it, without being of it. And it is through that detachment that we can empty the vessel of our heart in preparation for that which nourishes it and gives it life. By emptying our heart, we prepare it for its true nourishment:

God.

FOR THE LOVE OF THE GIFT

We all love gifts. We love the blessings that beautify our lives. We love our children, our spouses, our parents, our friends. We love our youth and we love our health. We love our homes, our cars, our money, and our beauty. But what happens when a gift becomes more than just a gift? What happens when a want becomes a need, a favor becomes a dependency? What happens when a gift is no longer only that?

What is a gift? A gift is something that did not come from us. A gift is given—and can be taken. We are not the original owners of a gift. A gift is also not necessary for our survival. It comes and goes. We want and love to receive gifts—but they are not necessary to our existence. We don't depend on them. We don't live to receive them and do not die if we don't. They are not our air or our food, but we love them. Who does not love a gift? Who does not love to receive many gifts? And we ask Al Kareem (The Most Generous) to never deprive us of His gifts. Yet, a gift is still not where we place our dependencies, nor do we die without them.

Remember that there are two places to hold something: in the hand or in the heart. Where do we hold a gift? A gift is not held in the heart. It is held in the hand. So when the gift is taken, the loss creates pain to the hand—but not to the heart. And anyone who has lived long enough in this life knows that the pain of the hand is not like the pain of the heart. The pain of the heart is to lose an object of attachment, addiction, dependency. That pain is like no other pain. It's not normal pain. And that pain is how we will know we just lost an object of attachment—a gift that was held in the wrong place.

The pain of the hand is also pain—but different. So different. The pain of the hand is to lose, but not something we are dependent upon. When a gift is taken out of the hand—or never given at all—we will feel the normal human pain of loss. We will grieve. We will cry. But the pain is only in the hand; our heart remains whole and beating. This is because the heart is only for God.

And God alone.

If we examine the things in our lives that cause us the most pain or fear, we can start to pinpoint which gifts have been stored in the wrong place. If not being able to get married, be with the person we want, have a child, find a job, look a certain way, get a degree, or reach a certain status has consumed us, we need to make a change. We need to shift where the gift is being stored; we need to move the gift out of our heart and back to our hand where it belongs.

We can love these things. It's human to love. And it's human to want the gifts we love. But our problem begins when we put the gift in our heart, and God in our hand. Ironically, we believe that we can live without God—but if we were to lose a gift, we crumble and can't go on.

As a result, we can easily put God aside, but our heart cannot live without the gift. In fact, we can even put God aside for the sake of the gift. So it becomes easy for us to delay or miss a prayer, but just don't deprive me of my work meeting, my movie, my outing, my shopping, my class, my party, or my basketball game. It's easy to take interest bearing loans or sell alcohol, just don't deprive me of my profit margin and prestigious career. Just don't deprive me of my brand new car, and over-the-top home. It's easy to have a haram relationship or date, but just don't deprive me of the one I 'love'. It's easy to take off, or not wear hijab—just don't deprive me of my beauty, my looks, my marriage proposals, or my image in front of people. It's easy to put aside the modesty that God says is beautiful, but don't deprive me of my skinny jeans—because society told me that's beauty.

This happens because the gift is in our heart, while Allah is in our hand. And what is in the hand can be put aside easily. What is in the heart, we cannot live without—and would sacrifice anything to have. But sooner or later we need to ask ourselves what it is that we really worship: The gift or the Giver? The beauty or the Source and Definition of Beauty? The provision or the Provider?

The creation or the Creator?

The tragedy of our choice is that we chain our necks with attachments, and then ask why we choke. We put aside our Real air, and then wonder why we can't breathe. We give up our only food, and then complain when we're dying of starvation. After all, we stick the knife in our chest and then cry because it hurts. So much. But what we have done, we have done to ourselves.

Allah says:

وما أصابكم من مصيبة فبما كسبت أيديكم ويعفو عن كثير

"And whatever affliction befalls you, it is on account of what your hands have wrought, and (yet) He pardons most (of your faults)." (Qur'an, 42:30)

Yes. What we have done, we have done to ourselves, but look how the ayah ends: "He pardons most." The word used here is ya'foo' from God's attribute

Al-A'foo. This denotes not just forgiving or pardoning, but completely erasing! So no matter how many times we stick that knife in our own chest, God can heal us—as if the stab had never occurred! Al Jabbar (the One who mends) can mend it.

If you seek Him.

But how foolish is the one who exchanges air for a necklace? He is the one who says, "Give me the necklace, and then you can take away my air after that. Suffocate me, but just make sure I'm wearing the necklace when I die." And the irony of it all is that it is the necklace itself that suffocates us. It is our own objects of attachment—the things we love more than God— that kill us.

Our problem began because we saw the gift as the air, instead of just that: a gift. So in our blindness, we became dependent on the gift, and put aside the Real air. As a result when the gift was taken back, or never given at all, we thought we could not go on. But, this was a lie that we told ourselves, until we believed it. It isn't true. There's only one loss that we can't recover from. There's only one reason we wouldn't be able to go on: If we lost God in our lives. The irony is that many of us have lost God in our lives and we think we're still alive. Our false dependencies on His gifts have deceived us, so much.

Only God is our survival. Not His gifts. God is our support and our only true necessity. Allah says:

أليس الله بكاف عبده ويخوفونك بالذين من دونه ومن يضلل الله فما له من هاد

"Is not God enough for His Servant? But they try to frighten thee with other (gods) besides Him! For such as God leaves to stray, there can be no guide." (Qur'an, 39:36)

We all have needs and we all have wants. Our true suffering begins when we turn our wants into needs, and our one true need (God) into a commodity we think we can do without. Our true suffering begins when we confuse the means and the End. God is the only End. Every other thing is the means. We will suffer the moment we take our eyes off the End and get lost in the means.

In fact, the true purpose of the gift itself is to bring us to God. Even the gift is a means. For example, does the Prophet ﷺ not say that marriage is half of deen? Why? If used correctly, few other parts of this life can have such a comprehensive effect on the development of one's character. You can read about qualities like patience, gratitude, mercy, humility, generosity, self-denial, and preferring another to yourself. But, you won't develop those qualities until you are put in a situation in which they are tested.

Gifts like marriage will be a means to bring you closer to God—so long as they remain a means, not an End. God's gifts will remain a means to Him, so long as they are held in the hand, not the heart. Remember that whatever lives in the heart controls you. It becomes what you strive for and are willing to sacrifice anything to have. And to keep. It becomes what you depend on at a fundamental level. It, therefore, must be something eternal, that never tires, and never breaks. It must, therefore, be something that never leaves. Only one thing is like that: The Creator.

PEACE ON A ROOFTOP

We've all had intense moments. For me, one such moment happened while standing on the rooftop of Masjid al-Haram. Above me was only sky, below me, the most beautiful view of the Kaba'a and an acute sign of Allah, this life, and the life to come. I was surrounded by an overwhelming crowd—that exists nowhere else on this earth—but, for me, it could have been that I was standing completely alone. With Allah.

I brought with me to that rooftop so much heartache, confusion, and doubt. I came with so much weakness, human frailty, and pain. Standing at a crossroads in my life, I brought with me fear of what was to come, and hope in what could be. So, as I stood on that roof, I remembered the story of Musa (*`alayhi assalam*—may Allah be pleased with him) standing at the Red Sea. His physical eyes saw nothing but a wall of water, entrapping him as an army approached; but his spiritual eyes saw only Allah, and a way out so certain it was as if he had already taken it. While the voices of his people—bereft of trust or hope—spoke only of being overtaken, Musa (as) did not waiver.

As I stood there, I heard the distant voices warning me of what was to come—but my heart heard only, "*Inna ma'iya rabee sa yahdeen*...Truly my Lord is with me, He will guide me through." (Qur'an, 26:62)

However seeing through the illusions of hardship, confusion and pain that surround us can only happen when we allow our heart to focus. The foundation of Islam is *tawheed* (Oneness), but *tawheed* is not just about saying that God is One. It is so much deeper. It is about the Oneness of purpose, of fear, of worship, of ultimate love for God. It is the oneness of vision and focus. It is to direct one's sight on one singular point, allowing everything else to fall into place.

One of the most beautiful traditions of the Prophet ﷺ captures this concept perfectly. He ﷺ said: "Whoever makes the Hereafter his preoccupation, then Allah places freedom from want in his heart, gathers his affairs, and *Dunya* (worldly life) comes to him despite being reluctant to do so. And whoever makes *Dunya* his preoccupation, then Allah places his poverty in front of his eyes, make his affairs scattered, and nothing of the *Dunya* comes to him except that which has been decreed for him." [At-Tirmidhi]

If you've ever seen a "magic eye" picture, you can see a wonderful metaphor of this truth. At first glance, the picture looks like nothing but a collection of shapes, with no order or purpose. But if you start by bringing the picture right up to your face, focusing your eye on one singular point, as you move the picture slowly away from your face, the picture suddenly becomes clear. However, as soon as you take your eyes off that singular point of focus, the picture disappears and again becomes nothing but a sea of shapes.

In the same way, the more we focus on the *dunya*, the more our matters become scattered. The more we run after the *dunya*, the more it runs away from us. The more we chase wealth, ironically, the more poverty we feel. If money is the focus, you will find that no matter how much money you have, you will always fear losing it. This preoccupation is poverty itself. That is why the Prophet ﷺ says about such people that poverty is always in front of their eyes. That is all they see. No matter how much they have, there is no contentment, only greed for more and fear of loss. But, for the ones who focus on Allah, the *dunya* comes to them, and Allah puts contentment in their hearts. Even if they have less, they feel rich, and are more willing to give from that wealth.

And when such people feel trapped by life, by financial hardship, by pain, by loneliness, by fear, by heartbreak, or sadness, all they have to do is turn to Allah, and He always makes a way out for them. Know that this is not some feel-good theory. It is a promise. A promise made by Allah Himself, who says in the Qur'an:

"...And for those who fear Allah, He (ever) prepares a way out, And He provides for him from (sources) he never could imagine. And if any one puts his trust in Allah, sufficient is (Allah) for him..." (Qur'an, 65:2-3)

Allah is sufficient for them. Allah is enough. For those who make Allah their primary concern, there is only peace, because whatever happens to them in this life it is good and accepted as the will of Allah. Imagine having only good in your life. That is the state of this type of believer, as the Prophet ﷺ says: "Wondrous are the believer's affairs. For him there is good in all his affairs, and this is so only for the believer. When something pleasing happens to him, he is grateful, and that is good for him; and when something displeasing happens to him, he is enduring (has *sabr*), and that is good for him." [Muslim]

And so in the heart of such a believer is a sort of paradise. That is the paradise that Ibn Taymiyyah, may Allah have mercy on his soul, spoke of when he said:

'Truly, there is a Heaven in this world, [and] whoever does not enter it, will not enter the Heaven of the next world.'

And in that heaven, complete peace is not something of a moment. It is a state, eternal.

THE OCEAN OF DUNYA

Yesterday, I went to the beach. As I sat watching the massive Californian waves, I realized something strange. The ocean is so breathtakingly beautiful. But just as it is beautiful, it is also deadly. The same spellbinding waves, which we appreciate from the shore, can kill us if we enter them. Water, the same substance necessary to sustain life, can end life, in drowning. And the same ocean that holds ships afloat can shatter those ships to pieces.

This worldly life, the dunya, is just like the ocean. And our hearts are the ships. We can use the ocean for our needs and as a means to get to our final destination. But the ocean is only that: a means. It is a means for seeking food of the sea. It is a means of travel. It is a means of seeking a higher purpose. But it is something which we only pass through, yet never think to remain in. Imagine what would happen if the ocean became our end—rather than just a means.

Eventually we would drown.

As long as the ocean's water remains outside the ship, the ship will continue to float and be in control. But what happens as soon as the water creeps into the ship? What happens when the dunya is not just water outside of our hearts, when the dunya is no longer just a means? What happens when the dunya enters our heart?

That is when the boat sinks.

That is when the heart is taken hostage and becomes a slave. And that is when the dunya—which was once under our control—begins to control us. When the ocean's water enters and overtakes a ship, that ship is no longer in control. The boat then becomes at the mercy of the ocean.

To stay afloat, we must view this world in exactly the same way, for Allah (swt) has told us that, "Verily in the creation of the heavens and the earth are signs for those who reflect." (Qur'an, 3:190) We live in the dunya, and the dunya is in fact created for our use. Detachment from dunya (zuhd) does not mean that we do not interact with this world. Rather, the Prophet ﷺ has taught us that we must:

Anas (ra) said: "Three people came to the houses of the wives of the Prophet ﷺ, may Allah bless him and grant him peace, to ask about how the Prophet ﷺ worshipped. When they were told, it was as if they thought it was little and said, 'Where are we in relation to the Messenger of Allah, may Allah bless him and grant him peace, who has been forgiven his past and future wrong actions?'" He said, "One of them said, 'I will pray all of every night'. Another said, 'I will fast all the time and not break the fast'. The other said, 'I will withdraw from women and never marry'. The Messenger of Allah came to them and said, 'Are you the ones who said such-and-such? By Allah, I am the one among you with the most fear and awareness of Allah, but I fast and break the fast, I pray and I sleep, and I marry women. Whoever disdains my sunnah is not with me.'" [Agreed upon]

The Prophet ﷺ did not withdraw from the dunya in order to be detached from it. His detachment was much deeper. It was the detachment of the heart. His ultimate attachment was only to Allah (swt) and the home with Him, for he truly understood the words of God:

"What is the life of this world but amusement and play? But verily the Home in the Hereafter,—that is life indeed, if they but knew." (Qur'an, 29:64)

Detachment does not even mean that we cannot own things of the dunya. In fact many of the greatest companions were wealthy. Rather, detachment is that we view and interact with the dunya for what it really is: just a means. Detachment is when the dunya remains in our hand—not in our heart. As 'Ali (ra) expressed beautifully, "Detachment is not that you should own nothing, but that nothing should own you."

Like the ocean's water entering the boat, the moment that we let the dunya enter our hearts, we will sink. The ocean was never intended to enter the boat; it was intended only as a means that must remain outside of it. The dunya, too, was never intended to enter our heart. It is only a means that must not enter or control us. This is why Allah (swt) repeatedly refers to the dunya in the Qur'an as a mata'a. The word mata'a can be translated as a "resource for transitory worldly delight". It is a resource. It is a tool. It is the path—not the destination.

And it is this very concept that the Prophet ﷺ spoke about so eloquently when he said:

"What relationship do I have with this world? I am in this world like a rider who halts in the shade of a tree for a short time, and after taking some rest, resumes his journey leaving the tree behind." (Ahmad, Tirmidhi)

Consider for a moment the metaphor of a traveler. What happens when you're traveling or you know that your stay is only temporary? When you're passing through a city for one night, how attached do you get to that place? If you know it's temporary, you'll be willing to stay at Motel 6. But would you like to live there? Probably not. Suppose your boss sent you to a new town to work on a limited project. Suppose he didn't tell you exactly when the project would end, but you knew that you could be returning home, any day. How would you be in that town? Would you invest in massive amounts of property and spend all your savings on expensive furniture and cars? Most likely not. Even while shopping, would you buy cart-loads of food and other perishables? No. You'd probably hesitate about buying any more than you need for a couple days—because your boss could call you back any day.

This is the mindset of a traveler. There is a natural detachment that comes with the realization that something is only temporary. That is what the Prophet ﷺ in his wisdom, is talking about in this profound hadith. He understood the danger of becoming engrossed in this life. In fact, there was nothing he feared for us more.

He ﷺ said, "By Allah I don't fear for you poverty, but I fear that the world would be abundant for you as it has been for those before you, so you compete for it as they have competed for it, so it destroys you as it has destroyed them." (Agreed upon)

The blessed Prophet ﷺ recognized the true nature of this life. He understood what it meant to be in the dunya, without being of it. He sailed the very same ocean that we all must. But his ship knew well from where it had come, and to where it was going. His was a boat that remained dry. He understood that the same ocean which sparkles in the sunlight will become a graveyard for the ships that enter it.

TAKE BACK YOUR HEART

No one likes to fall. And few people would ever choose to drown. But in struggling through the ocean of this life, sometimes it's so hard not to let the world in. Sometimes the ocean does enter us. The dunya does seep into our hearts.

And like the water that breaks the boat, when dunya enters, it shatters our heart. It shatters the boat. Recently, I was reminded of what a broken boat looks like, of what happens when you let everything in. I was reminded because I saw someone, just like me, fall in love too much with this life and seek to be filled by the creation. So the ocean of dunya shattered her boat, as it had shattered mine, and she fell out into the water. But she stayed down too long, and didn't know how to come back up or what to hold on to.

So she drowned.

If you allow dunya to own your heart, like the ocean that owns the boat, it will take over. You will sink down to the depths of the sea. You will touch the ocean floor. And you will feel as though you were at your lowest point. Entrapped by your sins and the love of this life, you will feel broken, surrounded by darkness. That's the amazing thing about the floor of the ocean. No light reaches it.

However, this dark place is not the end. Remember that the darkness of night precedes the dawn. And as long as your heart still beats, this is not the death of it. You don't have to die here. Sometimes, the ocean floor is only a stop on the journey. And it is when you are at this lowest point, that you are faced with a choice. You can stay there at the bottom, until you drown. Or you can gather pearls and rise back up—stronger from the swim and richer from the jewels.

If you seek Him, God can raise you up, and replace the darkness of the ocean, with the light of His sun. He can transform what was once your greatest weakness into your greatest strength, and a means of growth, purification and redemption. Know that transformation sometimes begins with a fall. So never curse the fall. The ground is where humility lives. Take it. Learn it. Breathe it in. And then come back stronger, humbler and more aware of your need for Him. Come back having seen your own nothingness and His greatness. Know that if you have seen that Reality, you have seen much. For the one who is truly deceived is the one who sees his own self—but not Him. Deprived is the one who has never witnessed his own desperate need for God. Reliant on his own means, he forgets that the means, his own soul, and everything else in existence are His creation.

Seek God to bring you back up, for when He does, He will rebuild your ship. The heart that you thought was forever damaged will be mended. What was shattered will be whole again. Know that only He can do this. Seek Him.

And when He saves you, beg forgiveness for the fall, feel remorse over it—but not despair. As Ibn ul Qayyim (ra) has said: "Satan rejoiced when Adam (peace be upon him) came out of Paradise, but he did not know that when a diver sinks into the sea, he collects pearls and then rises again."

There is a powerful and amazing thing about tawbah (repentance) and turning back to Allah (swt). We are told that it is a polish for the heart. What's amazing about a polish is that it doesn't just clean. It makes the object that is polished even shinier than it was before it got dirty. If you come back to God, seek His forgiveness, and refocus your life and heart on Him, you have the potential to be even richer than if you'd never fallen at all. Sometimes falling and coming back up gives you wisdom and humility that you may never otherwise have had. Ibn ul Qayyim (ra) writes:

"One of the Salaf (Pious Predecessors) said: "Indeed a servant commits a sin by which he enters Paradise; and another does a good deed by which he enters the Fire." It was asked: How is that? So he replied: "The one who committed the sin, constantly thinks about it; which causes him to fear it, regret it, weep over it and feel ashamed in front of his Lord—the Most High—due to it. He stands before Allah, broken-hearted and with his head lowered in humility. So this sin is more beneficial to him than doing many acts of obedience, since it caused him to have humility and humbleness—which leads to the servant's happiness and success—to the extent that this sin becomes the cause for him entering Paradise. As for the doer of good, then he does not consider this good a favor from his Lord upon him. Rather, he becomes arrogant and amazed with himself, saying: I have achieved such and such, and such and such. So this further increases him in self-adulation, pride and arrogance—such that this becomes the cause for his destruction."

Allah (swt) reminds us in the Qur'an to never lose hope. He says: "Say, 'O My servants who have transgressed against their souls [by sinning], despair not of the mercy of Allah. Indeed, Allah forgives all sins. Indeed, it is He who is the Forgiving, the Merciful,'" (Qur'an, 39:53).

And so, this is a call to all those who have become enslaved by the tyranny of the self, imprisoned in the dungeon of the nafs (self) and desires. It is a call to all those who have entered the ocean of dunya, who have sunk into its depths, and become trapped by its crushing waves. Rise up. Rise up to the air, to the Real world above the prison of the ocean. Rise up to your freedom. Rise up and come back to life. Leave the death of your soul behind you. Your heart can still live and be stronger and purer than it ever was. Does not the polish of tawbah remake the heart even more beautiful than it was? Remove the veil you have sewn with your sins. Remove the veil between you and Life, between you and Freedom, between you and Light—between you and God. Remove the veil and rise up. Come back to yourself. Come back to where you began. Come back Home. Know that when all the other doors have shut in your face, there is One that is always open. Always. Seek it. Seek Him and He will guide you through the waves of the cruel ocean, into the mercy of the sun.

This world cannot break you—unless you give it permission. And it cannot own you unless you hand it the keys—unless you give it your heart. And so, if you have handed those keys to dunya for a while—take them back. This isn't the End. You don't have to die here. Reclaim your heart and place it with its rightful owner:

God.

LOVE

Escaping the Worst Prison

When Sara met Ahmed, she immediately knew. He was everything she had always dreamed of. Meeting him was like watching the sun rise in the middle of a snowstorm. His warmth melted the cold. Soon, however, admiration turned to worship. Before she could understand what had happened, Sara had become a prisoner. She became a prisoner of her own desire and craving for that which she adored. Everywhere she looked, Sara saw nothing but him. Her greatest fear in life was displeasing him. He was all she could feel, and without him, happiness had no meaning. Leaving him made her feel as though her soul was being peeled from her very being. Her heart was consumed with only his face, and nothing felt closer to her than him. He became to her like the blood in her veins. The pain of existing without him was unbearable because there was no happiness outside of being with him.

Sara thought she was in love.

Sara had been through a lot in her life. Her father walked out on her when she was a teenager, she ran away from home when she was 16, and she battled drug and alcohol addictions. She even spent time in jail. However, all that pain combined could not compare to the pain she would come to know inside this new prison of her own making. Sara became a captive inside her own desires. It was this captivity that Ibn Taymiyyah radi Allahu 'anhu (may Allah be pleased with him) spoke of when he said, "The one who is (truly) imprisoned is the one whose heart is imprisoned from Allah and the captivated one is the one whose desires have enslaved him." (Ibn al-Qayyim, al-Wabil, pg 69)

The agony of Sara's worship of Ahmed was more intense than the agony of all her previous hardships. It consumed her, but never filled her. Like a parched man in the middle of a desert, Sara was desperately pursuing a mirage. But what was worse was the torturous result of putting something in a place only God should be.

Sara's story is so deep because it demonstrates a profound truth of existence. As human beings, we are created with a particular nature (fitrah). That fitrah is to recognize the oneness of God and to actualize this truth in our lives. Therefore, there is no calamity, no loss, no thing that will cause more pain than putting something equal to God in our lives or our hearts. Shirk on any level breaks the human spirit like no worldly tragedy could. By making the soul love, revere, or submit to something as it should only God, you are contorting the soul into a position that it, by its very nature, was never meant to be in. To see the reality of this truth, one only has to look at what happens to a person when they lose their object of worship.

On July 22, 2010, the Times of India reported that a 40-year-old woman committed suicide in her home by pouring kerosene over her body and setting herself on fire. The police said it appeared that the suicide was an "extreme step because she was unable to conceive a child over 19 years of marriage".

Only days earlier on July 16, police reported that a 22-year-old Indian man "committed suicide after his girlfriend left him".

Most people could sympathize with the pain of these people, and most would be heartbroken in the same position. But if having a child or a particular person in our life is our reason for being, something is terribly wrong. If something finite, temporary and fading becomes the center of our life, the raison d'etre (reason for existing), we will surely break. The imperfect objects that we place at our center will—by definition—fade, let us down, or pass away. And our break will occur as soon as it does. What happens if, while climbing a mountain, you hang on to a twig to hold all your weight? Laws of physics tell us that the twig, which was never created to carry such weight, will break. Laws of gravity tell us that it is then that you will most certainly fall. This is not a theory. It is a certainty of the physical world. This reality is also a certainty of the spiritual world, and we are told of this truth in the Qur'an. Allah says:

يا أيها الناس ضرب مثل فاستمعوا له إن الذين تدعون من دون الله لن يخلقوا ذبابا ولو اجتمعوا له وإن يسلبهم الذباب شيئا لا يستنقذوه منه ضعف الطالب والمطلوب

"People, here is an illustration, so listen carefully: those you call on beside God could not, even if they combined all their forces, create a fly, and if a fly took something away from them, they would not be able to retrieve it. How feeble are the petitioners and how feeble are those they petition!" (Qur'an, 22:73)

The message of this ayah (verse) is deeply profound. Every time you run after, seek, or petition something weak or feeble (which, by definition, is everything other than Allah), you too become weak or feeble. Even if you do reach that which you seek, it will never be enough. You will soon need to seek something else. You will never reach true contentment or satisfaction. That is why we live in a world of trade-ins and upgrades. Your phone, your car, your computer, your woman, your man, can always be traded in for a newer, better model.

However, there is a freedom from that slavery. When the object upon which you place all your weight is unshaking, unbreakable, and unending, you cannot fall. You cannot break. Allah explains this truth to us in the Qur'an when He says:

لا إكراه في الدين قد تبين الرشد من الغي فمن يكفر بالطاغوت ويؤمن بالله
فقد استمسك بالعروة الوثقى لا انفصام لها والله سميع عليم

"There is no compulsion in religion: true guidance has become distinct from error, so whoever rejects false gods and believes in God has grasped the firmest hand-hold, one that will never break. God is all hearing and all knowing." (Qur'an, 2:256)

When what you hold on to is strong, you too become strong, and with that strength comes the truest freedom. It is of that freedom that Ibn Taymiyyah, may Allah have mercy on him, said: "What can my enemies do to me? I have in my breast both my heaven and my garden. If I travel they are with me, never leaving me. Imprisonment for me is a chance to be alone with my Lord. To be killed is martyrdom and to be exiled from my land is a spiritual journey." (Ibn al-Qayyim, al-Wabil, p.69)

By making the one without flaw, end, or weakness the only object of his worship, Ibn Taymiyyah described an escape from the prison of this life. He described a believer whose heart is free. It is a heart free of the shackles of servitude to this life and everything in it. It is a heart that understands that the only true tragedy is the compromise of tawheed (the doctrine of the Oneness of God), that the only insurmountable affliction is the worship of anyone or anything other than the One worthy of worship. It is a heart that understands that the only true prison is the prison of replacing something with God. Whether that object is one's own desires, nafs (ego), wealth, job, spouse, children, or the love of one's life, that false deity will entrap and enslave you if you make it ultimate. The pain of that bondage will be greater, deeper, and longer lasting than any other pain which could be inflicted by all the tragedies of this life.

The experience of Prophet Yunus ʿalayhi sallatu wa sallam (may Allah send his peace and blessings upon him) is so crucial to internalize. When he was trapped in the belly of the whale, he had only one way out: turning completely to Allah, realizing Allah's oneness and his own human frailty. His duʿaʾ encapsulates this truth in such a profound way: "There is no God but You, glory be to You, I was wrong." (Qurʾan, 21:87)

Many of us are also trapped inside the belly of the whale of our own desires and objects of worship. It is our own selves which we become enslaved to. And that imprisonment is the result of putting anything where only God should be in our hearts. In so doing we create the worst and most painful of prisons; because while a worldly prison can only take away what is temporary and inherently imperfect, this spiritual prison takes away what is ultimate, unending and perfect: Allah and our relationship to Him.

IS THIS LOVE THAT I'M FEELING?

"Love is a serious mental disease." At least that's how Plato put it. And while anyone who's ever been 'in love' might see some truth to this statement, there is a critical mistake made here. Love is not a mental disease. Desire is.

If being 'in love' means our lives are in pieces and we are completely broken, miserable, utterly consumed, hardly able to function, and willing to sacrifice everything, chances are it's not love. Despite what we are taught in popular culture, true love is not supposed to make us like drug addicts.

And so, contrary to what we've grown up watching in movies, that type of all-consuming obsession is not love. It goes by a different name. It is hawa—the word used in the Qur'an to refer to one's lower, vain desires and lusts. Allah describes the people who blindly follow these desires as those who are most astray: "But if they answer you not, then know that they only follow their own lusts (hawa). And who is more astray than the one who follows his own lusts, without guidance from Allah?" (Qur'an, 28: 50)

By choosing to submit to our hawa over the guidance of Allah, we are choosing to worship those desires. When our love for what we crave is stronger than our love for Allah, we have taken that which we crave as a lord. Allah says: "Yet there are men who take (for worship) others besides Allah, as equal (with Allah): They love them as they should love Allah. But those of Faith are overflowing in their love for Allah." (Qur'an, 2:165)

If our 'love' for something makes us willing to give up our family, our dignity, our self-respect, our bodies, our sanity, our peace of mind, our deen, and even our Lord who created us from nothing, know that we are not 'in love'. We are slaves.

Of such a person Allah says: "Do you see such a one as takes his own vain desires (hawa) as his lord? Allah has, knowing (him as such), left him astray, and sealed his hearing and his heart, and put a cover on his sight. (Qur'an, 45: 23)

Imagine the severity. To have one's sight, hearing and heart all sealed. Hawa is not pleasure. It is a prison. It is a slavery of the mind, body and soul. It is an addiction and a worship. Beautiful examples of this reality can be found throughout literature. In Charles Dickens' Great Expectations, Pip exemplifies this point. In describing his obsession with Estella, he says: "I knew to my sorrow, often and often, if not always, that I loved her against reason, against promise, against peace, against hope, against happiness, against all discouragement that could be."

Dickens' Miss Havisham describes this further: "I'll tell you…what real love is. It is blind devotion, unquestioning self-humiliation, utter submission, trust and belief against yourself and against the whole world, giving up your whole heart and soul to the smiter—as I did!"

What Miss Havisham describes here is in fact real, but it is not real love. It is hawa. Real love, as Allah intended it, is not a sickness or an addiction. It is affection and mercy. Allah says in His book: "And of His signs is that He created for you from yourselves mates that you may find tranquility in them; and He placed between you affection and mercy. Indeed in that are signs for a people who give thought." (Qur'an, 30: 21)

Real love brings about calm—not inner torment. True love allows you to be at peace with yourself and with God. That is why Allah says: "that you may dwell in tranquility." Hawa is the opposite. Hawa will make you miserable. And just like a drug, you will crave it always, but never be satisfied. You will chase it to your own detriment, but never reach it. And though you submit your whole self to it, it will never bring you happiness.

So while ultimate happiness is everyone's goal, it is often difficult to see past the illusions and discern love from hawa. One fail-safe way, is to ask yourself this question: Does getting closer to this person that I 'love' bring me closer to—or farther from—Allah? In a sense, has this person replaced Allah in my heart?

True or pure love should never contradict or compete with one's love for Allah. It should strengthen it. That is why true love is only possible within the boundaries of what Allah has made permissible. Outside of that, it is nothing more than hawa, to which we either submit or reject. We are either slaves to Allah, or slaves to our hawa. It cannot be both.

Only by struggling against false pleasure, can we attain true pleasure. They are by definition mutually exclusive. For that reason, the struggle against our desires is a prerequisite for the attainment of paradise. Allah says: "But as for he who feared the position of his Lord and prevented the soul from [unlawful] inclination, then indeed, Paradise will be [his] refuge." (Qur'an, 79: 40-41)

LOVE IS IN THE AIR

Love is in the air!

…Or at least that's what advertisers want you to think in February. While it's nice to express your love often, Valentine's Day comes once a year, leaving you no choice but to do so or risk seeming heartless. For the owners of floral boutiques and chocolate shops, Eid comes in February.

Yet, even amidst such commercialized affections, one can hardly keep from thinking about those they love. And while we do so, we are inevitably faced with some pivotal questions.

I was reminded of some of those questions when I reflected on something a friend of mine had told me. She described how it felt to be with the person she loved. In her words, the whole world disappeared when they were together. The more I reflected on her statement, the more it affected me, and the more it made me wonder.

As humans, we are made to feel love and attachment towards others. This is part of our human nature. While we can feel this way about another human being, five times a day we enter into a meeting with our Lord and Creator. I wondered how often we ever felt the whole world disappear while in His presence. Can we really claim that our love for Allah is greater than our love for anyone and anything else?

So often we think that Allah only tests us with hardships, but this isn't true. Allah also tests with ease. He tests us with na'im (blessings) and with the things we love, and it is often in these tests that so many of us fail. We fail because when Allah gives us these blessings, we unwittingly turn them into false idols of the heart.

When Allah blesses us with money, we depend on the money rather than Allah. We forget that the source of our provision is not and never was the money, but rather it was the giver of that money. Suddenly we're willing to sell alcohol to avoid losing money in our business, or we need to take out loans with interest to feel secure. In so doing we are foolishly—and ironically—disobeying the Provider in order to protect the provision.

When Allah blesses us with someone that we love, we forget that Allah is the source of that blessing, and we begin to love that person as we should love

Allah. That person becomes the center of our world—all our concerns, thoughts, plans, fears, and hopes revolve only around them. If they are not our spouses, we are sometimes even willing to fall into haram just to be with them. And if they were to leave us, our whole world would crumble. So now, we have shifted our worship from the Source of the blessing to the blessing itself.

Allah says of such people: "And [yet], among the people are those who take other than Allah as equals [to Him]. They love them as they [should] love Allah. But those who believe are stronger in love for Allah." (Qur'an 2:165)

It is because of this tendency to lose sight after Allah has bestowed His blessings that He warns us in the Qur'an when He says: "Say, [O Muhammad], 'If your fathers, your sons, your brothers, your wives, your relatives, wealth which you have obtained, commerce wherein you fear decline, and dwellings with which you are pleased are more beloved to you than Allah and His Messenger and jihad in His cause, then wait until Allah executes His command. And Allah does not guide the defiantly disobedient people.'" (Qur'an, 9:24)

It is important to note that all the things listed in the above ayah (verse) are halal (permissible) to love and are, in fact, blessings in and of themselves. In fact, some of those blessings are signs of Allah. On the one hand, Allah says: "And of His signs is that He created for you from yourselves mates that you may find tranquility in them; and He placed between you affection and mercy. Indeed in that are signs for a people who give thought." (Qur'an 30:21)

But on the other hand, Allah warns: "O you who have believed, indeed, among your wives and your children are enemies to you, so beware of them." (Qur'an 64:14)

The warning in this ayah is critical. Our spouses and our children are listed here because they are among the blessings we love the most. And it is in that which you love most that you find the greatest test. So if conquering that test means seeing through a storm of greeting cards and roses to a greater love that awaits, then so be it. And when could that be more relevant?

Because after all, love is in the air.

THIS IS LOVE

And so there are some who spend their whole lives seeking. Sometimes giving, sometimes taking. Sometimes chasing, but often, just waiting. They believe that love is a place that you get to: a destination at the end of a long road. And they can't wait for that road to end at their destination. They are those hearts moved by the movement of hearts. Those hopeless romantics, the sucker for a love story, or any sincere expression of true devotion. For them, the search is almost a lifelong obsession of sorts. But, this tragic 'quest' can have its costs—and its gifts.

The path of expectations and the 'falling in love with love' is a painful one, but it can bring its own lessons. Lessons about the nature of love, this world, people, and one's own heart, can pave this often painful path. Most of all, this path can bring its own lessons about the Creator of love.

Those who take this route will often reach the knowledge that the human love they seek was not the destination. Some form of that human love, can be a gift. It can be a means, but the moment you make it the End, you will fall. And you will live your whole life with the wrong focus. You will become willing to sacrifice the Goal for the sake of the means. You will give your life to reaching a 'destination' of worldly perfection that does not exist.

And the one, who runs after a mirage, never gets there; but keeps running. And so too will you keep running, and be willing to lose sleep, cry, bleed, and sacrifice precious parts of yourself—at times, even your own dignity. You'll never reach what you're looking for in this life, because what you seek isn't a worldly destination. The type of perfection you seek cannot be found in the material world. It can only be found in God.

That image of human love that you seek is an illusion in the desert of life. So if that is what you seek, you'll keep chasing. But no matter how close you get to a mirage, you never touch it. You don't own an image. You can't hold a creation of your own mind.

Yet, you will give your whole life, still, to reaching this 'place'. You do this because in the fairy tale, that's where the story ends. It ends at the finding, the joining, and the wedding. It is found at the oneness of two souls. And everyone around you will make you think that your path ends there: at the place where you meet your soul mate, your other half—at the point in the path where you get married. Then and only then, they tell you, will you ever finally be complete. This, of course, is a lie because completion cannot be found in anything other than God.

Yet the lesson you've been taught since the time you were little—from every story, every song, every movie, every ad, every well-meaning auntie—is that you aren't complete otherwise. And if—God forbid—you are one of the 'outcasts' who haven't gotten married, or have been divorced, you are considered deficient or incomplete in some way.

The lesson you're taught is that the story ends at the wedding, and then that's when Jennah (paradise) begins. That's when you'll be saved and completed and everything that was once broken will be fixed. The only problem is, that's not where the story ends. That's where it begins. That's where the building starts: the building of a life, the building of your character, the building of sabr, patience, perseverance, and sacrifice. The building of selflessness. The building of love.

And the building of your path back to Him.

However if the person you marry becomes your ultimate focus in life, your struggle has just begun. Now your spouse will become your greatest test. Until you remove that person from the place in your heart that only God should be, it will keep hurting. Ironically, your spouse will become the tool for this painful extraction process, until you learn that there are places in the human heart made only by—and for—God.

Among the other lessons you may learn along this path—after a long road of loss, gain, failure, success, and so many mistakes—is that there are at least 2 types of love. There will be some people you love because of what you get from them: what they give you, the way they make you feel. This is perhaps the majority of love—which is also what makes much of love so unstable. A person's capacity to give is inconstant and changing. Your response to what you are given is also inconstant and changing. So if you're chasing a feeling, you'll always be chasing. No feeling is ever constant. If love is dependent on this, it too becomes inconstant and changing. And just like everything in this world, the more you chase it, the more it will run away from you.

But, once in a while, people enter your life that you love—not for what they give you—but for what they are. The beauty you see in them is a reflection of the Creator, so you love them. Now suddenly it isn't about what you're getting, but rather what you can give. This is unselfish love. This second type of love is the rarest. And if it is based in, and not competing with, the love of

God, it will also bring about the most joy. To love in any other way is to need, to be dependent, to have expectations—all the ingredients for misery and disappointment.

So for all those who have spent their life seeking, know that purity of any thing is found at the Source. If it is love that you seek, seek it through God. Every other stream, not based in His love, poisons the one who drinks from it. And the drinker will continue to drink, until the poison all but kills him. He will continue to die more and more inside, until he stops and finds the pure Source of water.

Once you begin to see everything beautiful as only a reflection of God's beauty, you will learn to love in the right way: for His sake. Everything and everyone you love will be for, through and because of Him. The foundation of such love is God. So what you hold onto will no longer be just an unstable feeling, a fleeting emotion. And what you chase will no longer be just a temporary high. What you hold, what you chase, what you love, will be God: the **only** thing stable and constant. Thereafter, everything else will be through Him. Everything you give or take or love or don't love, will be by Him. Not by your nafs. It will be for Him. Not for your nafs.

This means you will love what He loves and not love what He does not love. And when you do love, you will give to the creation—not for what you can get in return from them. You will love and you will give, but you will be sufficed from Him. And the one, who is sufficed by God, is the richest and most generous of all lovers. Your love will be by Him, for Him, and because of Him. That is the liberation of the self from servitude to any created thing. And that is freedom. That is happiness.

That is love.

FALL IN LOVE WITH THE REAL THING

It's never easy to let go. Or is it? Most of us would agree that there are few things harder than letting go of what we love. And yet, sometimes that's exactly what we have to do. Sometimes we love things that we can't have. Sometimes we want things that are not good for us. And sometimes we love what Allah does not love. To let go of these things is hard. Giving up something the heart adores is one of the hardest battles we ever have to fight.

But what if it didn't have to be such a battle? What if it didn't have to be so hard? Could there ever be an easy way to let go of an attachment? Yes. There is.

Find something better.

They say you don't get over someone until you find someone or something better. As humans, we don't deal well with emptiness. Any empty space must be filled. Immediately. The pain of emptiness is too strong. It compels the victim to fill that place. A single moment with an empty spot causes excruciating pain. That's why we run from distraction to distraction, and from attachment to attachment.

In the quest to free the heart, we speak a lot about breaking our false dependencies. But then there's always the question of 'how?' Once a false attachment has been developed, how do we break free? Often it feels too hard. We get addicted to things, and can't seem to let them go. Even when they hurt us. Even when they damage our lives and our bond with God. Even when they are so unhealthy for us. We just can't let them go. We are too dependent on them. We love them too much and in the wrong way. They fill something inside of us that we think we need...that we think we can't live without. And so, even when we struggle to give them up, we often abandon the struggle because it's too hard.

Why does that happen? Why do we have so much trouble sacrificing what we love for what God loves? Why can't we just let go of things? I think we struggle so much with letting go of what we love, because we haven't found something we love more to replace it.

When a child falls in love with a toy car, he becomes consumed with that love. But what if he can't have the car? What if he has to walk by the store every day, and see the toy he can't have? Every time he walks by, he would feel pain. And he may even struggle not to steal it. Yet, what if the child looks past the store window and sees a Real car? What if he sees the Real Ferrari? Would he still struggle with his desire for the toy? Would he still have to fight the urge to steal it? Or would he be able to walk right past the toy—the disparity in greatness annihilating the struggle?

We want love. We want money. We want status. We want this life. And like that child, we too become consumed with these loves. So when we can't have those things, we are that child in a store, struggling not to steal them. We are struggling not to commit haram for the sake of what we love. We are struggling to let go of the haram relationships, business dealings, actions, dress. We are struggling to let go of the love of this life. We are the stumbling servant struggling to let go of the toy…because it's all we see.

This whole life and everything in it is like that toy car. We can't let go of it because we haven't found something greater. We don't see the Real thing. The Real version. The Real model.

Allah (swt) says,

وما هذه الحياة الدنيا إلا لهو ولعب وإن الدار الآخرة لهي الحيوان لو كانوا

يعلمون

"What is the life of this world but amusement and play? But verily the Home in the Hereafter- that is life indeed, if they but knew." (Qur'an, 29:64)

When describing this life, Allah uses the Arabic word for 'life': الْحَيَاةُ. But, when describing the next life, Allah here uses the highly exaggerated term for life, الْحَيَوَانُ. The next life is the Real life. The Realer life. The Real version. And then Allah ends the ayah by saying "If they but knew". If we could see the Real thing, we could get over our deep love for the lesser, fake model.

In another ayah, God says:

بل تؤثرون الحياة الدنيا

والآخرة خير وأبقى

"But you prefer the worldly life, while the Hereafter is better and more enduring." (Qur'an, 87:16-17)

The Real version is better in quality (خَيْرٌ) and better in quantity (أَبْقَى). No matter how great what we love in this life is, it will always have some deficiency, in both quality (imperfections) and quantity (temporary).

This is not to say that we cannot have or even love things of this life. As believers, we are told to ask for good in this life and the next. But it is like the toy car and the real car. While we could have or even enjoy the toy car, we realize the difference. We understand fully that there is a lesser model (dunya: coming from the root word 'daniya', meaning 'lower') and there is the Real model (hereafter).

But how does that realization help us in this life? It helps because it makes the 'struggle' to follow the halal, and refrain from the haram easier. The more we can see the Real thing, the easier it becomes to give up the 'unreal'—when necessary. That does not mean we have to give up the 'unreal' completely, or all the time. Rather it makes our relationship with the lesser model (dunya) one in which if and when we *are* asked to give something up for the sake of what *is* Real, it is no longer difficult. If we are asked to refrain from a prohibition that we want, it becomes easier. If we are asked to be firm in a commandment that we don't want, it becomes easier. We become the matured child who likes to have the toy, but if ever asked to choose between the toy and the Real thing, see a 'no-brainer'. For example, many of the Prophet's ﷺ companions had wealth. But when the time came, they could easily give half or all of it for Allah's sake.

This focus also transforms what we petition for help or approval. If we're in desperate need of something, we will appeal to the servant—only when we don't see or know the King. But if we're on our way to meet that King and we run into His servant, we may greet the servant, be kind to the servant, even love the servant. Yet we will not waste time trying to impress the servant, when there is a King to impress. We will never waste effort appealing to the servant for our need, while the King is the One in control. Even if the King had given some authority to the servant, we'd know very well that the power to give and take rests ultimately with the King—and the King alone. *This knowledge comes only from knowing and seeing the King.* And this knowledge completely transforms how we interact with the servant.

Seeing the Real thing transforms the way we love. Ibn Taymiyyah (RA) discussed this concept when he said: "If your heart is enslaved by someone who is forbidden for him: One of the main causes for this miserable situation is turning away from Allah, for once the heart has tasted worship of Allah and sincerity towards Him, nothing will be sweeter to it than that, nothing will be more delightful or more precious. No one leaves his beloved except for another one he loves more, or for fear of something else. The heart will give up corrupt love in favor of true love, or for fear of harm."

One of our greatest problems as an ummah is as the Prophet ﷺ told us in a hadith: wahn (love of dunya and hatred of death). We've fallen in love with dunya. And anytime you are in love, it becomes next to impossible to get over that love or separate from it—until you are able to fall in love with something greater. It is next to impossible to dislodge this destructive love of dunya from our hearts, until we find something greater to replace it. Having found a greater love, it becomes easy to get over another one. When the love of God, His messenger and the Home with Him is really seen, it overpowers and dominates any other love in the heart. The more that love is seen, the more dominate it becomes. And thereby the easier it will be to really actualize the statement of Ibraheem (AS):

قل إن صلاتي ونسكي ومحياي ومماتي لله رب العالمين

"Say, 'Indeed, my prayer, my service of sacrifice, my living and my dying are for Allah, Lord of the worlds.'" (Qur'an, 6:162)

So in letting go, the answer lies in love. Fall in love. Fall in love with something greater. Fall in love with the Real thing. See the Mansion.

Only then, will we stop playing in the dollhouse.

A SUCCESSFUL MARRIAGE: THE MISSING LINK

"**Note:** This article is assuming a minimal level of mutual respect between spouse. By no means, should the concept of respect mean condoning abuse (physical, emotional or psychological). It is not sabr (patience) to accept abuse against yourself or your family. Allah (swt) says He does not approve of injustice. And neither should we."

"And among His signs is that He created for you mates from among yourselves that you may dwell in tranquility with them, and He has put love and mercy between you; verily, in that are signs for people who reflect." (Qur'an, 30:21)

We've all read this verse on countless marriage announcements. But how many have actualized it? How many of our marriages really embody that love and mercy described by Allah? What is going wrong when so many of our marriages are ending in divorce?

According to Dr. Emerson Eggerichs, author of Love & Respect: The Love She Most Desires; The Respect He Desperately Needs, the answer is simple. In his book, Eggerichs explains that extensive research has found that a man's primary need is for respect, while a woman's primary need is for love. He describes what he calls the "crazy cycle"—the pattern of argumentation that results when the wife does not show respect and the husband does not show love. He explains how the two reinforce and cause one another. In other words, when a wife feels that her husband is acting unloving, she often reacts with disrespect, which in turn makes the husband act even more unloving.

Eggerichs argues that the solution to the "crazy cycle" is for the wife to show unconditional respect to her husband and for the husband to show unconditional love to his wife. This means that a wife should not say that first her husband must be loving, before she will show him respect. By doing so, she will only bring about more unloving behavior. And a husband should not say that first his wife must be respectful before he will show her love. By doing so, he will only bring about more disrespectful behavior. The two must be unconditional.

When I reflected on this concept, I realized that looking at the Qur'an and prophetic wisdom, there are no two concepts more stressed with regards to the marital relationship.

To men, the Prophet ﷺ said,

"Take good care of women, for they were created from a bent rib, and the most curved part of it is its top; if you try to straighten it, you will break it, and if you leave it, it will remain arched, so take good care of women." (Bukhari & Muslim)

He has further stressed: "The most perfect believer in the matter of faith is one who has excellent behavior; and the best among you are those who behave best towards their wives." (Al-Tirmidhi)

The Prophet ﷺ has also said, "A believing man should not hate a believing woman; if he dislikes one of her characteristics, he will be pleased with another." (Muslim)

Allah says:

"…Live with them in kindness. For if you dislike them—perhaps you dislike a thing and Allah makes therein much good." (Qur'an, 4:19)

In these jewels of wisdom, men are urged to be kind and loving towards their wives. Moreover, they are urged to overlook their wife's faults when showing that kindness and love.

On the other hand, when addressing the wife, the focus is different. Why are women not told again and again to be kind and loving towards their husbands? Perhaps it is because unconditional love already comes naturally to women. Few men complain that their wives do not love them. But many complain that their wives do not respect them. And it is this sentiment which is most stressed in the Qur'an and sunnah, with regards to wives.

Respect can be manifest in a number of ways. One of the most important ways to show respect is the respect of one's wishes. When someone says, "I respect your advice," they mean "I will follow your advice." Respecting a leader, means doing what they say. Respecting our parents means not going against their wishes. And respecting one's husband means respecting his wishes. The Prophet ﷺ has said: "When any woman prays her five, fasts her month, guards her body and obeys her husband, it is said to her: 'Enter paradise from whichever of its doors you wish.'" [At-Tirmidhi]

Why are we as women told to respect and follow the wishes of our husbands? It is because men are given an extra degree of responsibility. Allah says: "Men are the protectors and maintainers [qawwamun] of women, because Allah has given the one more [strength] than the other, and because they support them from their means . . ." (Qur'an, 4:34)

But won't this unconditional respect towards one's husband put us, as women, in a weak, submissive position? Won't we set ourselves up to be taken advantage of and abused? Quite the contrary. The Qur'an, the prophetic example, and even contemporary research have proven the exact opposite. The more respect a woman shows her husband, the more love and kindness he will show her. And in fact, the more disrespect she shows, the harsher and unloving he becomes.

Similarly, a man may question why he should show kindness and love towards even a disrespectful wife. To answer this question, one only needs to look at the example of Omar Ibn ul-Khattab. When a man came to Omar (who was Khalifah at the time) to complain of his wife, he heard Omar's own wife yelling at him. While the man turned to leave, Omar called him back. The man told Omar that he had come to complain of the same problem that Omar himself had. To this Omar replied that his wife tolerated him, washed his clothes, cleaned his home, made him comfortable, and took care of his children. If she did all of this for him, how could he not tolerate her when she raised her voice?

This story provides a beautiful example for all of us—not only for the men. This story is a priceless illustration of tolerance and patience, which is essential for any successful marriage. Moreover, consider the reward in the hereafter for those who show patience: Allah says, "Only those who are patient shall receive their reward in full without reckoning (or measure)." (Qur'an, 39:10)

HARDSHIPS

THE ONLY SHELTER IN THE STORM

It's never easy to stand when the storm hits. As soon as it starts raining, lightening shortly follows. Dark clouds replace the sun and all you can see are the waves of an ocean, once calm, surrounding you. No longer able to find your way, you reach out for help.

You begin by calling the coast guard. No reply. You try again to redirect the boat. No use. You look for the lifeboat. It's gone. You reach for a life jacket. Torn. Finally after you've exhausted every means, you turn your face upward.

And ask God.

However, there's something completely unique about this moment. At this instant, you experience something you otherwise could only theorize about: true tawheed. Oneness. See, on shore, you may have called on God. But you called on Him along with so many others. You may have depended on God. But you depended on Him along with so many other handholds. But for this singular moment, everything else is closed. Everything. There is nothing left to call on. Nothing left to depend on. But Him.

And that's the point.

Do you ever wonder why when you're most in need, every door you seek of the creation remains closed? You knock on one, but it's slammed shut. So you go to another. It's also shut. You go from door to door, knocking, pounding on each one, but nothing opens. And even those doors you had once depended on, suddenly shut. Why? Why does that happen?

See, we humans have certain qualities which God knows well. We are constantly in a state of need. We are weak. But, we are also hasty and impatient. When we are in trouble, we will be pushed to seek assistance. And that's the design. Why would we seek shelter if it's sunny and the weather is nice? When does one seek refuge? It is when the storm hits. So Allah subahanahu wa ta'ala (exlated is He) sends the storm; He makes the need through a created situation, so that we will be driven to seek shelter.

But when we do seek assistance, because of our impatience, we seek it in what is near and what seems easy. We seek it in what we can see and hear and touch. We look for shortcuts. We seek help in the creation, including our own selves. We look for help in what seems closest. And isn't that exactly what dunya (worldly life) is? What seems near. The word 'dunya' itself means 'that which is lower'. Dunya is what seems closest. But, this is only an illusion.

There is something closer.

Think for a moment about what's nearest to you. If asked this question, many would say it is the heart and the self that are nearest. But, Allah (swt) says:

ولقد خلقنا الإنسان ونعلم ما توسوس به نفسه ونحن أقرب إليه من حبل

الوريد

"It was We Who created man, and We know what dark suggestions his nafs (self) makes to him: for We are nearer to him than (his) jugular vein." (Qur'an, 50:16)

In this verse, Allah (swt) begins by showing us that He knows our struggles. There is comfort in knowing that someone sees our struggles. He knows what our own self calls us to. But He is closer. He is closer than our own self and what it calls for. He is closer than our jugular vein. Why the jugular? What is so striking about this part of us? The jugular vein is the most important vein that brings blood to the heart. If severed, we die almost immediately. It is literally our lifeline. But Allah (swt) is closer. Allah (swt) is closer than our own life, than our own Self, than our own nafs. And He is closer than the most important pathway to our heart.

In another verse, Allah (swt) says:

يا أيها الذين آمنوا استجيبوا لله وللرسول إذا دعاكم لما يحييكم واعلموا أن الله

يحول بين المرء وقلبه وأنه إليه تحشرون

"O ye who believe! give your response to Allah and His Messenger, when He calleth you to that which will give you life; and know that Allah cometh in between a man and his heart, and that it is He to Whom ye shall (all) be gathered." (Qur'an, 8:24)

Allah (swt) knows we have a nafs. Allah knows we have a heart. Allah knows that these things drive us. However Allah tells us that He is closer to us than even these. So when we reach for other than Him, we are not only reaching for what is weaker, we are also reaching past what is closer, for what is further and more distant. Subhan Allah (Glory be to God).

So since this is our nature, as Allah (swt) knows best, He protects and redirects us by keeping all other doors of refuge closed during the storm. He knows that behind each false door is a drop. And if we enter it, we will fall. In His mercy, He keeps those false doors closed.

In His mercy, He sent the storm itself to make us seek help. And then knowing that we're likely to get the wrong answer, He gives us a multiple choice exam with only one option to choose from: the correct answer. The hardship itself is ease. By taking away all other hand-holds, all other multiple choice options, He has made the test simple.

It's never easy to stand when the storm hits. And that's exactly the point. By sending the wind, He brings us to our knees: the perfect position to pray.

SEEING YOUR HOME IN JENNAH: ON SEEKING DIVINE HELP

I know a story that isn't just a story. It begins with a woman who loved something more than the glitter of this life. She was a woman who never allowed herself to be defined or limited by her painful circumstances; she carried in her such a deep faith that she was willing to die for it. She was a queen, yet saw through the thrones and palaces of this world. She saw through her palace in this life, and looked instead to her palace in the next. But, for Asiyah, wife of Pharoah, this was not just a metaphoric glimpse of the heart. For Asiyah, her glimpse was a vision of her physical eyes.

Allah subhanahu wa ta`ala (exalted is He) says: "God sets forth an example for those who believe — the wife of Pharaoh who said: 'My Lord, build for me with Thee a house in heaven, and save me from the Pharaoh and his doings, and save me from an unjust people'."

I've heard the story of Asiyah countless times. And each time it strikes me. But it wasn't until recently that her story hit me for another reason entirely. A few months ago, I was facing a difficult test. And the beauty of having righteous, angel-like souls as your company is something priceless. When you are in difficulty, it only takes one text message, one status update on Facebook, one email to the Suhaibwebb listserve, and you have a whole army of beautiful souls praying for you. Subhan'Allah (glory be to Him).

So I made that request. I asked for the greatest gift any human being can give to another. I asked for sincere du`a', supplication. What I received overwhelmed me. I'll never forget that gift of Allah. I had people praying for me in qiyam (night prayer), while standing in front of the kabaa, while traveling, even while giving birth. I received so many du`a's, yet there was one that really hit me. It was just a simple text message, but it read: "May you be shown your Home in Jennah so that any hardship is made easy on you." I read it and it hit. It really hit.

And then I remembered the story of Asiyah, and suddenly realized something amazing. Asiyah was undergoing the most severe torture any person could imagine. Pharoah was the greatest tyrant ever to walk the earth. He wasn't just a ruler over her. He was her husband. And in her final moments, Pharoah began to brutally torture her. But something strange happened. Asiyah smiled. She was going through one of the most severe hardships any human being could experience, and yet she smiled.

How is that? How it is that she could be tortured and smile, and when we face a traffic jam, or someone looks at us the wrong way, we can't handle it? How is it that Prophet Ibrahim (as) ʿalayhi sallatu wa sallam (may Allah send His peace and blessings on him) was faced with one of the greatest calamities, and yet the fire felt cool for him? Why do some people who have nothing find no reason to complain, while others who have 'everything' find nothing but reasons to complain? How is it that sometimes we have more patience with the big challenges in life than we do with the everyday small ones?

I used to think calamites were hard because certain things are just objectively difficult to bear. I thought there was a master list, a standard hierarchy of difficulty. The death of a loved one, for example, is always harder to bear than getting a traffic ticket. It seems obvious enough. It seems obvious.

But, it's also wrong.

A calamity of any type is not hard to bear because the calamity itself is difficult. The measure of ease or difficulty in hardship is on a different scale—an unseen scale. Whatever I face in life will be easy or difficult, not because it is easy or difficult. The ease or difficulty is based only on the level of Divine help. Nothing, nothing is easy, unless God makes it easy on me. Not a traffic jam. Not a paper cut. And nothing is hard if Allah makes it easy on me. Not illness, not death, not being thrown into fire, or tortured by a tyrant.

Ibn Attaillah al-Sakandari said it beautifully: "Nothing is difficult if you seek it through your Lord, and nothing is easy if you seek it through yourself."

Ibrahim (as) was thrown into fire. God willing none of us will ever face such a trial in this life. But there is not a person who won't get thrown into some sort of emotional, psychological or social fires in their life. And don't think for a moment that God cannot make those fires cool for us. Asiyah was being physically tortured, but Allah showed her a home in Jennah. So she smiled. Our physical eyes will not see jennah in this life. But, if Allah wills, the vision of our heart can be shown the home with Him, so that every difficulty is made easy. And maybe we too can smile, even in those times.

So the problem is not the trial itself. The problem is not the hunger or the cold. The problem is whether we have the provision needed when that hunger and cold come. And if we do, neither hunger nor cold will touch us. It won't hurt. The problem is only when the hunger comes and we don't have food. The problem is when the snow storm hits and we have no shelter.

Indeed Allah sends the trials, whereby we may be purified, strengthened and returned to Him. But, know for sure that with that hunger, thirst and cold,

Allah also sends the food, the water and the shelter. Allah sends the test, but with it He can send the sabr (patience), and even the rida (contentment) to withstand it. Yes, Allah (swt) sent Adam down to this world where he would have to struggle and face trials. But he also promised His Divine help. The Qur'an tells us: "He said: [Allah] said, 'Descend from Paradise—all, [your descendants] being enemies to one another. And if there should come to you guidance from Me—then whoever follows My guidance will neither go astray [in the world] nor suffer [in the Hereafter]'". (Qur'an, 20: 123)

Perhaps one of my favorite du'a's is that of the Prophet ﷺ at Taif. Bloody and covered with wounds, he called out to His Lord: "I seek refuge in the light of Your Face by which all darkness is dispelled and every affair of this world and the next is set right."

Indeed Allah does test those whom He loves and He tests in proportion to the level of faith. But so too does Allah send His Divine assistance whereby any test can be made easy and any fire can be made cool. So too can Allah send His Divine assistance whereby a single glimpse of His light and the home with Him can make us smile—even in the midst of the flames of trial.

HURT BY OTHERS: HOW TO COPE AND HEAL

When I was growing up, the world was a perfect place. The only problem was that it wasn't. I used to believe that everything could always be 'fair'. To me that meant no one should ever be wronged, and if they were, justice must be served. I fought hard for the way I believed things should be. However in my struggle, I overlooked a fundamental truth about this life. In my childish idealism, I failed to understand that this world is inherently imperfect. We, as humans, are inherently imperfect. So **we will** always mess up. And in those mess-ups, we will inevitably hurt others, knowingly and unknowingly, intentionally and unintentionally. The world would not always be fair.

Does that mean we stop struggling against injustice, or give up on Truth? Of course not, but it means we must not hold this world—and others—to an unrealistic standard. But that's not always easy. How do we live in a world so flawed, where people let us down, and even our own family can break our heart? And perhaps, hardest of all, how do we learn to forgive when we have been wronged? How do we become strong, without being hard, and remain soft, without being weak? When do we hold on, and when can we let go? When does caring too much, become too much? And is there such a thing as loving more than we should?

To begin to find these answers, we have to first take a step outside our own lives. We need to examine whether we are the first or the last to feel pain or be wronged. We need to look at those who came before us, to study their struggles, and their triumphs. And we need to recognize that growth never comes without pain, and success is only a product of struggle. That struggle almost always includes withstanding and overcoming the harms inflicted by others.

Recalling the shining examples of our prophets will remind us that our pain is not isolated. Remember that Prophet Nuh (as) was abused by his people for 950 years. The Quran tells us: "Before them the People of Noah rejected (their apostle): they rejected Our servant, and said, 'Here is one possessed!', and he was driven out." (Qur'an, 54:9) Nuh was abused so much that he finally called on his Lord: "I am one overcome: do Thou then help (me)!" (Qur'an, 54:10)

Or we can call to mind how the Prophet ﷺ was pelted with stones, until he bled, and how the companions were beaten and starved. All of this harm was at the hands of others. Even the angels understood this aspect of human nature—before we even came to be. When Allah told the angels that He would create humanity, their first question was about this harmful potential of humans. Allah tells us: "Behold, thy Lord said to the angels: 'I will create a vicegerent (humanity) on earth.' They said: 'Wilt Thou place therein one who will make mischief therein and shed blood?'" (Qur'an, 2:30)

This potential of humanity to commit horrific crimes against each other is a sad reality of this life. And yet many of us are so blessed. Most of us have not had to face the type of calamities that others have endured throughout time. Most of us will never have to watch as our families are tortured or killed. And yet, there are few of us who could say we have never been hurt, in one way or another, at the hands of someone else. So although most of us will never have to know the feeling of starving to death or standing helpless as our homes are destroyed, most of us will know what it means to cry from a wounded heart.

Is it possible to avoid this? To some degree, I think it is. We can never avoid all pain, but by adjusting our expectation, our response, and our focus, we can avoid much devastation. For example, putting our entire trust, reliance, and hope in another person is unrealistic and just plain foolish. We have to remember that humans are fallible and therefore, our ultimate trust, reliance, and hope should only be put in Allah. Allah says: "...whoever rejects evil and believes in Allah has grasped the most trustworthy hand-hold that never breaks. And Allah is Hearing and Knowing of all things." (Qur'an, 2:256) Knowing that Allah is the only hand-hold that never breaks will save us from much unneeded disappointment.

Yet, this is not to say that we should not love or that we should love less. It is how we love that is important. Nothing should be our ultimate object of love, except Allah. Nothing should come before Allah in our hearts. And we should never come to a point where we love something, other than Allah, in such a way, that it would be impossible to continue life without it. This type of 'love' is not love, but actually worship and it causes nothing but pain.

But what happens when we've done all that and still we have been hurt or wronged by others—as will also inevitably happen? How can we do what is the hardest? How can we learn to forgive? How can we learn to mend our scars and continue being good to people, even when they are not good to us?

In the story of Abu Bakr radi Allahu 'anhu (may Allah be pleased with him), is a beautiful example of exactly that. After his daughter, 'Ayesha (r), was slandered in the worst way, Abu Bakr (r) found out that the man who began the rumor was Mistah, a cousin who Abu Bakr had been supporting financially. Naturally Abu Bakr withheld the charity he had been giving the slanderer. Soon after, Allah revealed the following ayah: "Let not those among you who are endued with grace and amplitude of means resolve by oath against helping their kinsmen, those in want and those who migrated in the path of Allah. Let them forgive and overlook. Do you not wish that Allah should forgive you? Indeed Allah is oft-Forgiving, most Merciful." (Qur'an, 24:22) Upon hearing this ayah, Abu Bakr resolved that he did want Allah's forgiveness, and so he not only continued to give the man money, he gave him more.

This type of forgiveness is at the very heart of being a believer. In describing these believers, Allah says: "And who shun the more heinous sins and abominations; and who, whenever they are moved to anger, readily forgive." (Qur'an, 42:37)

The ability to readily forgive should be driven by an awareness of our own flaws and mistakes towards others. But most of all, our humility should be driven by the fact that we wrong Allah every single day of our lives, when we sin. Who are we compared to Allah? And yet, Allah, Master of the universe, forgives by day and by night. Who are we to withhold forgiveness? If we hope to be forgiven by Allah, how can we not forgive others? It is for this reason that the Prophet ﷺ teaches us: "Those who show no mercy to others will have no mercy shown to them by Allah." [Muslim]

This hope for Allah's mercy should motivate our own desire to forgive and to one day enter the only world that really is perfect.

THE DREAM OF LIFE

It was only a dream. For a moment, it overtakes me. Yet the suffering I feel in my nightmare is only an illusion. Temporary. Like the blink of an eye. But, why do I dream? Why do I have to feel that loss, fear, and sadness in my sleep?

On a greater scale, it's a question that has been asked throughout time. And for many people, the answer to that question has determined their path to—or away from—faith. Faith in God, faith in life's purpose, faith in a higher order or a final destination has often all rested upon how this singular question has been answered. And so, to ask this question is to ask about life, in the most ultimate way.

Why do we suffer? Why do 'bad' things happen to 'good' people? How could there be a God if innocent children starve and criminals run free? How can there be an all-loving, all-powerful deity who would allow such misfortunes to happen?

And if God is indeed Just and Good, shouldn't only *good* things happen to good people and only *bad* things happen to bad people?

Well, the answer is: yes. Absolutely. Only good things *do* happen to good people. And only bad things happen to bad people. Why? Because God IS the Most Just and the Most Loving. And He has no deficiency in His knowledge or understanding.

The problem is that *we* do have deficiencies in knowledge and understanding.

See, to understand the statement "only good things happen to good people and only bad things happen to bad people", we must first define 'good' and 'bad'. And although there are as many definitions of good and bad as there are people, a comprehensive understanding exists. For example, most people would agree that to succeed in achieving my desired purpose or goal in a particular matter would be 'good'. While on the other hand, failing to achieve my intended purpose or aim would be bad. If my aim is to gain weight because I am dangerously underweight, becoming heavier would be good. If, on the other hand, my aim is to lose weight because I am harmfully overweight, becoming heavier would be *bad*. The same event could be good or bad, depending on my intended purpose. So 'good' in my eyes rests on the achievement of my personal aim. And ultimate 'Good' rests on the achievement of my ultimate aim.

But what is my aim?

That brings us to the fundamental question of purpose as it relates to the greater Reality of existence. There are essentially two distinct worldviews when it comes to purpose in life. The first worldview holds that this life is the Reality, the final destination and ultimate goal of our endeavors. The second worldview holds that this life is only a bridge, a *means* that stands as nothing more than a glimpse in the context of God's infinite Reality.

For those in the first group, this life is everything. It is the End to which all actions strive. For those in the second group, this life tends towards zero. Why? Because, in comparison to infinity, even the largest number becomes zero. Nothing. Like a fleeting dream.

These distinct worldviews directly affect the question of purpose. See, if one believes that this life is the Reality, the final destination, the goal of all endeavors, the purpose of life would be to maximize pleasure and gain in *this* life. In that paradigm, 'bad' things ARE in fact happening to 'good' people every single second. Within that paradigm, people reach the conclusion that there is no justice and therefore either there is no God or God is not Just (*wa athu billah*, I seek refuge in God). It's like a person who concludes that there must be no God because they had a bad dream. But why don't we give the experiences of our dreams much weight? After all, some dreams *are* horrifying to live through—and very often do happen to 'good' people. In our dreams, do we not experience extreme terror or bliss? Yes. But why doesn't it matter?

Because put in context of our *real* life, it is nothing.

In the second world view (the Islamic paradigm) the purpose of creation is *not* maximizing pleasure and gain in a life that is nothing more than a dream. In that world view, life's purpose is defined by God who tells us: "I have not created jinn and humans (for any purpose) except to worship me," (Qur'an, 51:56).

It is important to note the special construction of this statement. It begins with a negation: 'I have not created jinn and humans (for any purpose) [...]'. First Allah *subhanahu wa ta'ala* (exalted is He) negates ALL other purposes before He states the one and only, singular purpose: 'except to worship Me'. This means that as a believer I know that there is *no other* purpose of my existence except to know, love and get closer to God. This is the one and only reason why I was created. And this is the most essential realization, as it defines everything else I do or believe. It defines all things around me, and everything I experience in life.

So returning to the meaning of 'good' and 'bad', we find that anything that brings us closer to our ultimate purpose is Good and anything that takes us away from our ultimate purpose is Bad, in an ultimate sense. In a relative sense, for those whose goal is this material world, worldly things define their 'good' and 'bad'. For them, things like gaining wealth, status, fame, or property is necessarily 'good'. Losing wealth, status, fame, or property is necessarily 'bad'. So in that paradigm, when an innocent person loses every material possession they own, this is a 'bad' thing happening to a 'good' person. But that is the illusion that comes as a result of a flawed worldview. When the lens itself is distorted, so too is the image seen through it.

For those of the second worldview, anything that brings us closer to our purpose of nearness to God's love is good; and anything that takes us away from that purpose is bad. Therefore, winning a billion dollars may be the greatest calamity ever to happen to me if it takes me away from God—my ultimate purpose. On the other hand, losing my job, all my wealth, and even falling ill, may in fact be the greatest blessing ever given to me if it brings me closer to God—my ultimate purpose. This is the Reality that is spoken about in the Qur'an when Allah (swt) says:

كتب عليكم القتال وهو كره لكم وعسى أن تكرهوا شيئا وهو خير لكم وعسى أن تحبوا شيئا وهو شر لكم والله يعلم وأنتم لا تعلمون

"It may happen that you hate a thing which is good for you, and it may happen that you love a thing which is bad for you. Allah knows, you know not." (Qur'an 2:216)

As a believer, my criterion is no longer gain or loss in a material sense. My criterion is something higher. What I have or do not have in a worldly sense is only relevant in as much as it brings me closer or farther from my Aim: God. This *dunya* (life) becomes nothing more than that dream that I experience for a moment and then awaken from. Whether that dream was good or bad for me, depends only on my state once I awaken.

And so on the ultimate scale there is perfect justice. God only gives good (nearness to Him) to good people, and bad (distance from Him) to bad people. The greatest good is nearness to God, in this life and the next. And it is only 'good' people who are blessed with this. That is why the Prophet ﷺ has said: "Strange is the case of a believer, there is good for him in everything—and this is only for the believer. If a blessing reaches him, he is grateful to God, which is good for him, and if an adversity reaches him, he is patient which is good for him." (Muslim)

As this *hadith* (record of the sayings or actions of the Prophet ﷺ) explains, whether something is good or bad is not defined by how it appears externally. "Goodness", as explained by this *hadith*, is defined by the good *internal* state that it produces: patience and gratitude—both manifestations of peace with and nearness to God.

On the other hand, the greatest calamity is distance from God—in this life and the next. And it is only 'bad' people who are punished with this. What such 'distanced' people have, or do not have of wealth or status or property or fame is only an illusion—no more real or important than having, or not having, these things in the greatest dream, or the worst nightmare.

Of these illusions Allah (swt) says: "Nor strain your eyes in longing for the things We have given for enjoyment to parties of them, the splendor of the life of this world, through which We test them: but the provision of thy Lord is better and more enduring." (Qur'an, 20:131)

The enduring life is the one that begins once we awaken from this world. And it is in that awakening that we realize…

It was only a dream.

CLOSED DOORS AND THE ILLUSIONS THAT BLIND US

Yesterday my 22 month old sought to exercise his independence. After climbing out of his car seat, he wanted to shut the car door like a big boy, so I stood there watching over him. Realizing that if I left him to shut the door, his little head would have gotten slammed in the process, I lifted him away, and shut the door myself. This devastated him, and he broke down in tears. How could I prevent him from doing what he so badly wanted to do?

Watching the incident, a strange thought crossed my mind. I was reminded of all the times this had happened to us in life—when we want something so badly, but Allah does not allow us to have it. I was reminded of all the times we, as adults felt this same frustration when things just wouldn't work out the way we so desperately wanted them to. And then suddenly, it was so clear. I had only taken my son away from the door to protect him. But he had no idea. In the midst of his mourning, he had no idea that I had actually saved him. And just as my son wept in his naivety and innocence, so often we too bemoan events that have actually saved us.

When we miss a plane, lose a job, or find ourselves unable to marry the person we want, have we ever stopped to consider the possibility that it may have been for our own good? Allah tells us in the Qur'an: "…But perhaps you hate a thing and it is good for you; and perhaps you love a thing and it is bad for you. And Allah Knows, while you know not." (Qur'an, 2:216)

Yet it is so difficult to look beyond the surface of things. It takes great strength to see beyond the illusions, to a deeper truth—which we may or may not understand. Just as my son could not understand how my depriving him of what he most wanted at that moment was in fact my looking out for him, we are often just as blind.

As a result, we end up staring indefinitely at the closed doors of our lives, and forget to notice the ones that have opened. When we can't marry the person we had in mind, our inability to look beyond may even blind sight us from someone who is in fact better for us. When we don't get hired, or we lose something dear to us, it's hard to take a step back and notice the bigger picture. Often Allah takes things away from us, only to replace them with something greater.

Even tragedy may happen in this way. One can imagine few calamities more painful than the loss of a child. And yet, even this loss could happen to save us and give us something greater. The Prophet ﷺ said:

If the child of a servant (of Allah) dies, Allah says to His Angels: 'Have you taken the child of My servant?'

The Angels reply: 'Yes.'

Allah says to them: 'Have you taken the fruit of his heart?'

They reply: 'Yes.'

Then Allah says to them: 'What did my servant say?'

The Angels reply: 'He praised Allah and said: 'To Allah do we return.'

Allah tells them: 'Build a home for my servant in Paradise and call it Baytul Hamd (the House of Praise).' [Tirmidhi]

When Allah takes something as beloved from us as a child, it may be that He has taken it in order to give us something greater. It may be because of that loss, that we are admitted into paradise—an eternal life with our child. And unlike our life here, it is an everlasting life where our child will have no pain, fear, or sickness.

But in this life, even our own sicknesses may not be what they seem. Through them Allah may be in fact purifying us of our sins. When the Prophet ﷺ was suffering from a high fever, he said: "No Muslim is afflicted with any harm, even if it were the prick of a thorn, but that Allah expiates his sins because of that, as a tree sheds its leaves." [Bukhari]

In another hadith the Prophet ﷺ explains that this applies even to sadness and worry. He says: "Whenever a Muslim is afflicted with a hardship, sickness, sadness, worry, harm, or depression—even a thorn's prick, Allah expiates his sins because of it." [Bukhari]

Or consider the example of poverty. Most people without wealth would never consider that a possible blessing. But for the people around Qarun, it was. Qarun was a man who lived at the time of Prophet Musa (as) who Allah had endowed with such great wealth, which even the keys to his wealth was itself wealth. The Qur'an says: "So he came out before his people in his adornment. Those who desired the worldly life said, 'Oh, would that we had like what was given to Qarun. Indeed, he is one of great fortune.'" (Qur'an 28:79)

But Qarun's wealth had made him arrogant, ungrateful, and rebellious against Allah. Allah says: "And We caused the earth to swallow him and his home. And there was for him no company to aid him other than Allah, nor was he of those who [could] defend themselves. And those who had wished for his position the previous day began to say, 'Oh, how Allah extends provision to whom He wills of His servants and restricts it! If not that Allah had conferred favor on us, He would have caused it to swallow us. Oh, how the disbelievers do not succeed!'" (Qur'an, 28:81-82) After seeing the fate of Qarun, the same people became grateful that they had been saved from his wealth.

But perhaps there is no better example of this lesson, than in the story of Musa and Al-Khidr that we are told about in Surat Al-Kahf. When Prophet Musa (as) was traveling with Al-Khidr (who commentators say was an angel in the form of a man), he learned that things are often not what they seem, and that the wisdom of Allah cannot always be understood from the surface. Al-Khidr and Prophet Musa (as) came upon a town whereupon Al-Khidr began to damage the boats of the people.

On the surface, this action would seem to have been harmful to the poor owners of the boats. However, Al-Khidr later explains that he was in fact protecting the people, and saving the boats for them. Allah tells us in the Qur'an: "[Al-Khidhr] said, 'This is parting between me and you. I will inform you of the interpretation of that about which you could not have patience. As for the ship, it belonged to poor people working at sea. So I intended to cause defect in it as there was after them a king who seized every [good] ship by force.'" (Qur'an 18:78-79)

In damaging the boats, Al-Khidr was actually protecting the people by making the boats undesirable to the king who had been seizing them by force. And sometimes in life, that's exactly what happens. In order to save us, something is taken away from us, or given to us in a way we don't want. And yet to us—as it did to a 22 month old boy—it looks only like a closed door.

PAIN, LOSS AND THE PATH TO GOD

I still remember the desperation. In the deep disappointment which often follows self-reflection, I turned to my Creator to plead. I turned to plead— but not for what can be measured, bought, sold, or traded. It was desperation for a truer currency. With my flaws suddenly made open to me, I became desperate to be liberated from the tyranny of my own *nafs* (lower desires). I became desperate to be a better person.

And so, handing my heart to Allah (swt), I prayed that I might be purified. And while I had always held to firm faith that God is the Hearer of prayers, I never imagined when—or how—that prayer would be answered.

Soon after that prayer, I experienced one of the most difficult periods of my life. During the experience, I braced myself, and prayed for guidance and strength. But never did I see any connection to my previous prayer. It was not until that time had passed, and reflecting on it, I realized how I had grown. Suddenly, I remembered my prayer. Suddenly I felt that the difficulty was itself the answer to the prayer I had made so desperately.

The words of Rumi explain beautifully: "When someone beats a rug with a stick, he is not beating the rug—his aim is to get rid of the dust. Your inward is full of dust from the veil of '*I*'-ness, and that dust will not leave all at once. With every cruelty and every blow, it departs little by little from the heart's face, sometimes in sleep and sometimes in wakefulness."

So often we experience things in life, and yet never see the connections between them. When we are given a hardship, or feel pain, we often fail to consider that the experience may be the direct cause or result of another action or experience. Sometimes we fail to recognize the direct connection between the pain in our lives and our relationship with Allah (swt).

That pain and adversity serves many purposes in life. Times of hardship can act as both an indication as well as a cure, for our broken relationship with our Creator.

Times of difficulty test our faith, our fortitude and our strength. During these times, the level of our *iman* becomes manifest. Adversity strips away our masks, revealing the truth behind mere declaration of faith. Hardships separate those whose declaration is true from those who are false.

Allah says: "Do the people think that they will be left to say, 'We believe' and they will not be tested? But We have certainly tested those before them, and Allah will surely make evident those who are truthful, and He will surely make evident the liars." (Qur'an, 29:2-3).

Hardships test us. Hardships can also be a blessing and a sign of Allah's love.

The Prophet Muhammad ﷺ said: "Whenever Allah wills good for a person, He subjects him to adversity." [Bukhari]

And yet most people cannot fathom how adversity could possibly be good. Many do not recognize that hardship is in fact a purifier, which brings people back to their Lord. What happens to the arrogant who are suddenly put in a situation they cannot control? What happens to a man who finds himself stranded on the ocean in the middle of a storm? What happens when the ship that is 'unsinkable' becomes the tale of the Titanic?

These perceived misfortunes are in fact wake up calls. They humble. They shake. They remind us of how small we are, and how Great God is. And in that way they awaken us from the slumber of our deceptions, our heedlessness, our wandering, and bring us back to our Creator. Hardships strip away the veil of comfort from our eyes, and remind us of what we are and where we're going.

Allah (swt) says: "...And We tested them with good [times] and bad that perhaps they would return [to obedience]." (Qur'an, 7:168) In another *ayah*, Allah (swt) explains: "Whenever We sent a prophet to a town, We took up its people in suffering and adversity, in order that they might learn humility." (Qur'an, 7:94)

This lesson in humility purifies the human soul so much so that Allah (swt) comforts the believers in the Qur'an, assuring them that any pain they encounter is intended to elevate and honor them. He says:

"If a wound hath touched you, be sure a similar wound hath touched the others. Such days (of varying fortunes) We give to men and men by turns: that Allah may know those that believe, and that He may take to Himself from your ranks Martyr-witnesses (to Truth). And Allah loveth not those that do wrong." (Qur'an, 3:140-142)

It is that very battle to purify the self which is the essence of the upward path to God. It begins with self-sacrifice, and is paved by the sweat of struggle. It is this path, which God describes when He says: "Oh mankind! Verily you are ever toiling on towards your Lord—painfully toiling—but you shall meet Him." (Qur'an, 84:6)

A BELIEVER'S RESPONSE TO HARDSHIP

For Muslims, now is a time of turmoil. Sometimes, it's difficult not to feel despair. Many of us are wondering, why is this happening to us? How could this happen when we've done nothing wrong? How can we be facing so much discrimination in the very country founded on "freedom", "liberty" and "justice" for all?

While all these thoughts are natural, we need to look beyond them. We need to look through the illusion for a moment, into the Reality that stands behind it. We must refocus our sight, if we are to see the Truth beyond this hologram.

That truth is one of the most oft-repeated lessons in the Qur'an and prophetic teachings. That fundamental truth is this: **Everything in this life is a test.**

Allah says in the Qur'an: "It is He who created death and life in order to test you, which of you are best in deeds. And He is the Exalted in Might, Oft-Forgiving." (Qur'an, 67:2)

Here we are told that the very purpose for which life and death were created: to test us. Think for a moment about an emergency siren. What is its purpose? The siren is an indication and a warning that something harmful is coming. If we hear it, we naturally panic. But what happens when they need to test the siren? What happens when it's just a drill to see how we will react? The test siren sounds exactly the same, but it is "only a test." Although it looks, sounds, and feels real, it is not. It is only a test. And we're reminded of that again and again throughout the test.

This is exactly what Allah tells us about this life. It is going to look, sound, and feel very, very real. At times it's going to scare us. At times it's going to make us cry. At times it's going to make us flee, instead of standing firm—even more firm—in our places. But this life and everything in it is only a test. It is not actually real. And like that test of the emergency broadcast system; it is training us for what *is* real. It is training us for the Reality beyond the test siren.

Now, what would happen if the coming of that test siren was not even a surprise? What if each and every household were given notification that the test was coming? Consider for a moment the notification of Allah (swt) to us (exalted is He):

لتبلون في أموالكم وأنفسكم ولتسمعن من الذين أوتوا الكتاب من قبلكم
ومن الذين أشركوا أذى كثيرا وإن تصبروا وتتقوا فإن ذلك من عزم الأمور

"The present world is only an illusory pleasure: you are sure to be tested through your possessions and persons; you are sure to hear much that is hurtful from those who were given the Scripture before you and from those who associate others with God. If you are steadfast and mindful of God that is the best course." (Qur'an, 3:186)

Now imagine that in addition to these notifications, we were given knowledge of countless other communities who were similarly tested. Allah says:

أم حسبتم أن تدخلوا الجنة ولما يأتكم مثل الذين خلوا من قبلكم مستهم
البأساء والضراء وزلزلوا حتى يقول الرسول والذين آمنوا معه متى نصر الله ألا
إن نصر الله قريب

"Do you suppose that you will enter the Garden without encountering what those before you encountered? They were afflicted by misfortune and hardship, and they were so shaken that even [their] messenger and the believers with him cried, 'When will God's help arrive?' Truly, God's help is near." (Qur'an, 2:214)

So not only was the siren predicted—it was not new. Suppose our community was told that we are not unique. So after all of that, how then would we react once the test siren came? Well, if it's a drill, there's no shock or disbelief. We don't panic. We don't even become distressed.

But we do act.

And here's the crucial part. Who are we acting for? Who is testing us? Who is watching, really? CNN, C-Span, the American public? No. They're all a part of the illusion; all a part of the test. They're all just a creation of the test. We act for one judge and one judge alone. We act for the only true Reality (al-Haqq). We act because we know He is watching, and He is the only One who will judge this test.

Once we realize this fundamental truth, something dramatic happens. As soon as we internalize that it is only a test, our questions drastically change. Instead of asking: "How could this be happening?" "Why is it so unfair?" our questions become: "How should I react?" "How should I pass this test?" "What am I meant to learn?" "How should I see through this illusion, to the creator of the one who's hurting me, the one who's oppressing me, and the test itself?" "How can we as a community use this test to bring us closer to our final destination, God?" and "How can we use this test to fulfill the purpose for which it was *created* - a tool to bring us nearer to Him?" *Allahu akbar* (God is Great).

The beauty of the tests of Allah (swt) is that after notifying us that they're coming, He gives us the exact recipe for succeeding in them: *Sabr* (patience) and *Taqwa* (God-consciousness).

Allah (swt) says: "The present world is only an illusory pleasure: you are sure to be tested through your possessions and persons; you are sure to hear much that is hurtful from those who were given the Scripture before you and from those who associate others with God. *If you are steadfast (have sabr) and mindful of God (have taqwa), that is the best course.*" (Qur'an, 3:185-186)

In another verse, Allah (swt) emphasizes these same two necessary components for averting any harm as a result of the schemes against us:

إن تمسسكم حسنة تسؤهم وإن تصبكم سيئة يفرحوا بها وإن تصبروا وتتقوا

لا يضركم كيدهم شيئا إن الله بما يعملون محيط

"They grieve at any good that befalls you [believers] and rejoice at your misfortunes. But if you are steadfast and conscious of God, their scheming will not harm you in the least: God encircles everything they do." (Qur'an, 3:120)

As part of our manual for success in these trials, Allah (swt) also tells us how those before us reacted when they were tested:

"Men said to them: 'A great army is gathering against you, so fear them', But it (only) increased them in Faith and they said: 'God is enough for us, and He is the best protector.' And they returned with Grace and bounty from Allah. No harm ever touched them: For they followed the good pleasure of God. And God's favor is great indeed. It is only the Evil one who urges you to fear his followers; do not fear them, but fear Me, if you are true believers." (Qur'an, 3:173-175)

In another passage Allah (swt) tells us:

"Many prophets have fought, with large bands of godly men alongside them who, in the face of their sufferings for God's cause, did not lose heart or weaken or surrender: God loves those who are steadfast (have sabr). All they said was, 'Our Lord, forgive us our sins and our excesses. Make our feet firm, and give us help against the disbelievers', and so God gave them both the rewards of this world and the excellent rewards of the Hereafter: God loves those who do good. You who believe, if you obey the disbelievers, they will make you revert to your old ways and you will turn into losers. No indeed! It is God who is your protector: He is the best of helpers." (Qur'an, 3:146-150)

Allah (swt) conveys these stories to us, so that we can learn from the response of those who passed before us. And their response was this: "God is enough for us, and He is the best of protectors." Their response was: "Our Lord, forgive us our sins and our excesses. Make our feet firm, and give us help against the disbelievers." Their response was not to look *at* the test. Their response was to look *through* it. They looked through the illusion and focused on the One behind it: God. They realized that, not only was Allah (swt) the giver of the test, He was the only one who could save them from it. And so they beseeched Him for His help through repentance, *sabr*, and perfecting their moral character (*taqwa*).

But most reassuring of all, Allah (swt) Himself comforts the believers and promises them success:

"Do not lose heart, nor fall into despair—you have the upper hand, if you are true believers. If a wound hath touched you, be sure a similar wound hath touched the others. Such days (of varying fortunes) We give to men and men by turns: that Allah may know those that believe, and that He may take to Himself from your ranks Martyr-witnesses (to Truth). And Allah loves not those that do wrong. Allah's object also is to purify those that are true in Faith and to deprive of blessing those that resist Faith. Did you think that you would enter Heaven without Allah testing those of you who fought hard (In His Cause) and remained steadfast?" (Qur'an, 3:139-142)

Once we change our lens with which we see our lives, our internal and external response drastically changes. When the righteous before us were tested, it only increased them in faith and obedience. The Qur'an recounts: "When the Believers saw the Confederate forces, they said: 'This is what Allah and his Messenger had promised us, and Allah and His Messenger told us what was true.' And it only added to their faith and their zeal in obedience." (Qur'an, 33:22)

However until we change that lens, we will never move beyond, "how could this happen to us" to realize the true purpose of the test itself: a created tool to purify, strengthen and bring us closer to the Creator of you, me and all our enemies.

THIS LIFE: A PRISON OR PARADISE?

I was at the airport. Standing in the security line, I awaited my ritual interrogation. As I stood there, I looked over at a little girl with her mother. The girl was crying. She was clearly sick. The mother reached into a bag to give the girl some medicine. I was struck by how miserable the little girl looked and suddenly I saw something. I felt as though I was looking at someone who was trapped. This innocent, pure soul was imprisoned by a worldly body that had to get sick, feel pain, and suffer.

And then I was reminded of the *hadith* in which the Prophet ﷺ said: "This world is a prison for the believer and a paradise for the disbeliever" (Sahih Muslim). And for the first time, I understood it very differently than I had before. I think many people misinterpret this hadith to mean that the disbelievers get to enjoy themselves in this life, while the believers have to be restricted in this life by *haram* (prohibited) and *halal* (permitted), and have to wait until the next life to enjoy themselves. Or perhaps, some think it means that this life is miserable for the believer, while it is bliss for the disbeliever.

But, I don't think that's it at all.

And suddenly I felt as though I was seeing the reality of this *hadith* in the little girl. I saw what looked like a soul imprisoned because it belongs to another world—a better world, where it *doesn't* have to get sick.

But what happens when it's the opposite? What happens when the soul already thinks it's in paradise? Would that soul ever want to be somewhere else? Somewhere better? No. It is *exactly* where it wants to be. To that soul, there *is* no 'better'. When you're in a paradise, you can't imagine being anywhere greater. You yearn for nothing else. Nothing more. You are satisfied, content with where you are. That is the condition of the disbeliever. Allah says:

$$\text{إن الذين لا يرجون لقاءنا ورضوا بالحياة الدنيا واطمأنوا بها والذين هم عن}$$

$$\text{آياتنا غافلون}$$

"Indeed, those who do not expect the meeting with Us and are satisfied with the life of this world and feel secure therein and those who are heedless of Our signs." (Qur'an, 10:7)

For the disbelieving soul, this inevitably painful, disappointing and temporary world IS their paradise. It's all they know. Imagine if a world where you have to fall, bleed and eventually die was the only paradise you knew. Imagine the agony of that.

The one who does not believe that there is any place better—who believes that this world is the best it can get—will become very impatient when this life isn't perfect. They are quickly angered and quickly devastated because this life was supposed to be a paradise. They don't realize there is something greater. And so this is all they want. This is all they strive for. Every effort, every ability, every opportunity, every gift endowed to them by their creator, is employed for the sake of seeking this life—of which nothing will come to them except what is written.

Their soul is attached to the worldly body because it thinks that body is the only paradise it has. Or will ever have. So it doesn't want to let go. At any price, it wants to hold on. To take the soul from its 'paradise' at death is the greatest torture possible. God describes the death of the disbelievers as a *tearing* of the soul from the body. Allah says:

$$\text{والنازعات غرقا}$$

"By the (angels) who tear out (the souls of the wicked) with violence…" (Qur'an, 79:1)

It tears because that soul doesn't want to leave. It believed it was already in its heaven. It didn't realize that there is something greater. So much greater.

For the believing soul, it's different. The believer is in prison—not paradise. Why? What is a prisoner? A prisoner is someone who is trapped. A prisoner is kept from his home, stuck, while he wishes to be somewhere better. The worldly body is a prison for the believer, not because this life is miserable for the believing soul, but because that soul yearns to be somewhere greater. It yearns to be Home. No matter how wonderful this life is for a believer, it is a prison compared to the Perfect life that awaits them. This soul's attachment is to God and the *true* paradise with Him. It wants to be there. But this worldly life is what keeps that soul from returning—for a while. It is the barrier, the prison. Although, the heart of a believer holds the only true paradise of this life, the soul still seeks what is beyond. The soul still seeks its Home, but this soul must remain in the bars of the body for an appointed term. It must 'do the time', before it can be released to go Home. The attachment of the believing soul is not to the imprisoning body. When the sentence is over and a captive is told he can go Home, he would never hold on to the prison bars. So Allah describes the death of the believer very differently. God says:

والناشطات نشطا

"By those (angels) who gently take out (the souls of the believers)…" (Qur'an, 79:2)

The believing soul slips easily out of the body. Its 'prison sentence' is over and now it's going Home. It doesn't hold on like the disbelieving soul that thought it was already at the best it can get.

And so I could not imagine a more perfect analogy than the one used by our beloved Prophet ﷺ. Indeed this life is a prison for the believer and a paradise for the disbeliever. We will all be called back by the very same caller. The question is, will we live our life so that when that call comes we hold on to the bars of the prison? Or will we live so that the call is a call of release. A call back Home.

RELATIONSHIP WITH
THE CREATOR

SALAH: LIFE'S FORGOTTEN PURPOSE

Man has taken many journeys throughout time. But there is one journey that nobody has ever taken.

Nobody—except one.

On a vehicle no man has ever ridden, through a path no soul has ever seen. To a place no creation has ever before set foot. It was the journey of one man to meet the Divine. It was the journey of Muhammad ﷺ, Prophet of God, to the highest heaven.

It was al Israa wal Miraaj (the magnificent journey).

On that journey Allah took his beloved Prophet ﷺ to the seventh heaven—a place not even angel Gibreel could enter. In the Prophet's ﷺ mission on earth, every instruction, every commandment was sent down through angel Gibreel. But, there was one commandment that was not. There was one commandment so important, that rather than sending angel Gibreel down with it, Allah brought the Prophet ﷺ up to Himself.

That commandment was salah (prayer). When the Prophet ﷺ was first given the command to pray, it was to be fifty times in a day. After asking Allah to make it easier, the commandment was eventually reduced to five times a day, with the reward of the fifty.

Reflecting upon this incident scholars have explained that the process of going from fifty to five was a deliberate one, intended to teach us the true place salah should hold in our lives. Imagine for a moment actually praying fifty times a day. Would we be able to do anything else but pray? No. And that's the point. What greater way than that to illustrate our life's true purpose? As if to say, salah is our real life; all the rest that we fill our day with…just motions.

And yet, we live as if it's exactly the opposite. Salah is something we squeeze into our day, when we find time—if that. Our 'lives' don't revolve around salah. Salah revolves around our 'lives'. If we're in class, salah is an afterthought. If we're at the mall, the Macy's sale is more urgent. Something is seriously wrong when we put aside the very purpose of our existence in order to watch a basketball game.

And that is for those who even pray at all. There are those who have not only put aside their life's purpose, they have abandoned it completely. What we often don't realize about the abandonment of salah is this: No scholar has ever held the opinion that committing zina (fornication) makes you a disbeliever. No scholar has ever held the opinion that stealing, drinking or taking drugs makes you a disbeliever. No scholar has even claimed that murder makes you a non-Muslim. But, about salah, some scholars have said he who abandons it, is no longer Muslim. This is said based on a hadith such as this one:

"The covenant between us and them is prayer, so if anyone abandons it, he has become a disbeliever." [Ahmad]

Imagine an act so egregious that the Prophet ﷺ would speak about it is such a way. Consider for a moment what satan did wrong. He didn't refuse to believe in Allah. He refused to make one sajdah. Just one. Imagine all the sajdahs we refuse to make.

Consider the seriousness of such a refusal. And yet, think how lightly we take the matter of salah. Salah is the first thing we will be asked about on the Day of Judgment, and yet it is the last thing that is on our mind. The Prophet ﷺ said: "The first thing which will be judged among a man's deeds on the Day of Resurrection is the Prayer. If this is in good order then he will succeed and prosper but if it is defective then he will fail and will be a loser." [Tirmidhi]

On that Day, the people of paradise will ask those who have entered Hell-fire, why they have entered it. And the Qur'an tells us exactly what their first response will be: "What led you into Hell Fire? They will say: 'We were not of those who prayed.'" (Qur'an, 74:42-43)

How many of us will be among those who say, "we were not of those who prayed, or we were not of those who prayed on time, or we were not of those who made prayer any priority in our lives?" Why is it that if we're in class or at work or fast asleep at the time of fajr and we need to use the restroom, we make time for that? In fact, the question almost sounds absurd. We don't even consider it an option not to. And even if we were taking the most important exam of our lives, when we need to go, we will go. Why? Because the potentially mortifying consequences of not going, makes it a non-option.

There are many people who say they don't have time to pray at work or school, or while they're out. But how many have ever said they don't have time to go to the bathroom, so while out, at work or school have opted instead to just wear Depends? How many of us just don't feel like waking up at Fajr time if we need to use the bathroom, and choose instead to wet our bed? The truth is we'll get out of bed, or leave class, or stop work, to use the bathroom, but not to pray.

It sounds comical, but the truth is, we put the needs of our body above the needs of our soul. We feed our bodies, because if we didn't, we'd die. But so many of us starve our souls, forgetting that if we are not praying our soul is dead. And ironically, the body that we tend to is only temporary, while the soul that we neglect is eternal.

SALAH AND THE WORST KIND OF THEFT

The only sad part of finding the straight path is when you lose it. There are many ways to fall, but no fall is more tragic than a fall in one's deen. Sometimes it's a sister who decided to take off her hijab and live a different type of life, other times it's a brother who was once active in the community, but got caught up with the wrong crowd. But, with each story, somehow, somewhere along the line, our brothers and sisters fell so far.

Sadly, these stories are not uncommon. Sometimes we can't help but look at them and wonder: How? Why? We wonder how someone who was so straight could have gotten so far off the path.

In wondering this, we often don't realize that the answer may be simpler than we think. People fall into all types of sin, but there is one sin many of these people have in common. There is one common denominator for most individual who lives a life full of sin. Whether that person was once on the straight path and fell, or whether that person was never on that path at all, one thing is likely. That person had to first abandon, minimize, put aside, or ignore their salah (prayer) before they were able to fall.

If one is praying, but continues to live a life full of sin, that salah is likely only the action of limbs—not heart or soul. See, there is a crucial characteristic of salah that is often overlooked. Besides being a sacred meeting with our creator, salah is a protection of the realest kind. Allah says, "Recite, [O Muhammad], what has been revealed to you of the Book and establish prayer. Indeed, prayer prohibits immorality and wrongdoing, and the remembrance of Allah is greater. And Allah knows that which you do." (Qur'an, 29:45)

When someone decides to abandon salah, they are also abandoning this protection. It is important to remember that this abandonment of salah often does not happen all at once, but rather in stages. It begins by delaying prayers out of their specified times and then combining one prayer with another. Soon it turns into missing the prayer all together. Before you know it, not praying becomes the norm.

Meanwhile something else is happening that cannot be seen. With every delayed or missed prayer, a hidden battle is being waged: The battle of shaytan. By abandoning the salah, the human being has put down the armor given to them by Allah, and has entered the battle field with no protection.

Now shaytan can have full reign. Of this truth Allah says: "And whoever is blinded from remembrance of the Most Merciful—We appoint for him a devil, and he is to him a companion." (Qur'an, 43:36)

So it should be of no surprise to anyone that neglecting salah becomes the very first step in the path to a lower life. Those who have fallen off the path need only to look back at where it began; and they will find that it began with the salah. The same is perfectly true the other way around. For those who wish to turn their lives around, it begins by focusing on and perfecting the salah. Once you put salah back as the priority—before school, work, fun, socializing, shopping, TV, ball games—only then can you turn your life around.

The irony of this truth is that many people are deceived into thinking that they need to first turn their life around, before they can start to pray. This thinking is a dangerous trick of shaytan, who knows that it is the salah itself which will give that person the fuel and guidance necessary to turn their life around. Such a person is like a driver whose car is on empty, but insists on finishing the journey before filling up on gas. That person won't be going anywhere. And in the same way, such people end up in the same place for years: not praying, and not changing their lives. Shaytan challenged them, and won.

In so doing, we have allowed him to steal from us what is priceless. Our homes and our cars are so precious to us, that we would never think to leave them unprotected. So we pay hundreds of dollars on security systems to keep them safe. And yet our deen is left unprotected, to be stolen by the worst of thieves—a thief who has vowed God Himself to be our relentless enemy until the end of time. A thief who is not simply stealing some carved metal with a Mercedes symbol on it. A thief who is stealing our eternal soul and everlasting ticket to Paradise.

A SACRED CONVERSATION

There is a time of night when the whole world transforms. During the day, chaos often takes over our lives. The responsibilities of work, school, and family dominate much of our attention. Other than the time we take for the five daily prayers, it is hard to also take time out to reflect or even relax. Many of us live our lives at such a fast pace, we may not even realize what we're missing.

However there is a time of night when work ends, traffic sleeps, and silence is the only sound. At that time—while the world around us sleeps—there is One who remains awake and waits for us to call on Him. We are told in the hadith qudsi:

> "Our Lord descends during the last third of each night to the lower heaven, and says: 'Is there anyone who calls on Me that I may respond to him? Is there anyone who asks Me that I may give unto him? Is there anyone who requests My Forgiveness that I may forgive him?'" (Bukhari and Muslim)

One can only imagine what would happen if a king were to come to our door, offering to give us anything we want. One would think that any sane person would at least set their alarm for such a meeting. If we were told that at exactly one hour before dawn a check for $10,000,000 would be left at our doorstep, would we not wake up to take it?

Allah subhanahu wa ta'ala (exalted is He) has told us that at this time of night, just before dawn, He will come to His servants. Imagine this. The Lord of the universe has offered us a sacred conversation with Him. That Lord waits for us to come speak with Him, and yet many of us leave Him waiting while we sleep in our beds. Allah (swt) comes to us and asks what we want from Him. The Creator of all things has told us that He will give us whatever we ask.

And yet we sleep.

There will come a day when this veil of deception will be lifted. The Qur'an says: "[It will be said], You were certainly in unmindfulness of this, and We have removed from you your cover, so your sight, this Day, is sharp." (Qur'an, 50:22).

On that Day, we will see the true reality. On that Day, we will realize that two rak'at (units) of prayer were greater than everything in the heavens and the earth. We will realize the priceless check that was left on our doorstep every night as we slept. There will come a day when we would give up everything under the sky just to come back and pray those two rak'at.

There will come a day when we would give up everything we ever loved in this life, everything that preoccupied our hearts and minds, every mirage we ran after, just to have that conversation with Allah. But on that Day, there will be some from whom Allah (swt) will turn away… and forget, as they had once forgotten Him.

The Qur'an says: "He will say, 'My Lord, why have you raised me blind while I was [once] seeing?' [Allah] will say, 'Thus did Our signs come to you, and you forgot them; and thus will you this Day be forgotten.'" (Qur'an, 20:125-126) In Surat al-Mu'minoon, Allah says: "Do not cry out today. Indeed, by Us you will not be helped." (Qur'an, 23:65)

Can you imagine for a moment what these ayat (verses) are saying? This is not about being forgotten by an old friend or classmate. This is about being forgotten by the Lord of the worlds. Not hellfire. Not boiling water. Not scalded skin. There is no punishment greater than this.

And as there is no punishment greater than this, there is no reward greater than what the Prophet ﷺ describes in the following hadith:

> "When those deserving of Paradise would enter Paradise, the Blessed and the Exalted would ask: Do you wish Me to give you anything more? They would say: Hast Thou not brightened our faces? Hast Thou not made us enter Paradise and saved us from Fire? He would lift the veil, and of things given to them nothing would be dearer to them than the sight of their Lord, the Mighty and the Glorious." [Sahih Muslim]

However, one does not need to wait until that Day to know the result of this nighttime meeting with Allah (swt). The truth is, there are no words to describe the overwhelming peace in this life from such a conversation. One can only experience it to know. Its effect on one's life is immeasurable. When you experience qiyam, the late night prayer, the rest of your life transforms. Suddenly, the burdens that once crushed you become light. The problems that were irresolvable become solved. And that closeness to your Creator, which was once unreachable, becomes your only lifeline.

THE DARKEST HOUR AND THE COMING OF THE DAWN

According to a well-stated proverb, the darkest hour is just before the dawn. And although astronomically the darkest point is much earlier, the truth of this proverb is metaphoric—but in no way less real.

So often we find that the darkest times in our lives are followed by the most precious. Often, it is at the moment when everything looks broken that something least expected lifts us and carries us through. Did not Prophet Ayoub (as) lose everything one by one, before it was all given back and more?

Yes. For Prophet Ayoub (as), the night was real. And for many of us, it seems to last forever. But Allah does not allow an endless night. In His mercy, he gives us the sun. Yet there are times when we feel our hardships won't cease. And maybe some of us have fallen to such a spiritual low in our deen (religion) that we feel disconnected from our Creator. And maybe for some of us, it's so dark, we don't even notice.

But like the sun that rises at the end of the night, our dawn has come. In His infinite mercy, Allah has sent the light of Ramadan to erase the night. He has sent the month of the Qur'an so that He might elevate us and bring us from our isolation to His nearness. He has given us this blessed month to fill our emptiness, cure our loneliness, and end our soul's poverty. He has sent us the dawn that we might find from darkness—light. Allah says,

$$هو الذي يصلي عليكم وملائكته ليخرجكم من الظلمات إلى النور وكان بالمؤمنين رحيما$$

"He it is Who sends blessings on you, as do His angels, that He may bring you out from the depths of Darkness into Light: and He is Full of Mercy to the Believers." (Qur'an, 33:43)

And this mercy extends to all who seek it. Even the most hardened sinner is told to never lose hope in God's infinite mercy. God says in the Qur'an:

$$قل يا عبادي الذين أسرفوا على أنفسهم لا تقنطوا من رحمة الله إن الله يغفر الذنوب جميعا إنه هو الغفور الرحيم$$

"Say: "O my Servants who have transgressed against their souls! Despair not of the Mercy of Allah. For Allah forgives all sins: for He is Oft-Forgiving, Most Merciful." (Qur'an, 39:53)

Allah is the Owner of mercy, and there is no time when that mercy is showered more upon us than in the blessed month of Ramadan. The Prophet has said regarding Ramadan: "Its beginning is mercy, its middle is forgiveness, and its ending is liberation from the Hellfire." (Ibn Khuzaymah, al-Sahih)

Every moment of Ramadan is a chance to come back to Allah. Whatever we are now going through in our lives is often a direct result of our own actions. If we are humiliated, or feel low, it is our own sins which have lowered us. It is only by Allah that we can ever hope to be elevated. If we are consistently unable to wake up for Fajr, or if we find it increasingly difficult to stay away from haram (the forbidden), we must examine our relationship with Allah. Most of all, we must never be deceived. We must never allow ourselves to think that anything in this world succeeds, fails, is given, taken, done, or undone without Allah. It is only by our connection to our Creator that we rise or fall in life, in our relationship with our world—and with all of humanity.

But unlike humanity, our Creator doesn't hold grudges. Imagine receiving a clean slate. Imagine having everything you ever regret doing erased completely. Ramadan is that chance. The Prophet ﷺ told us: "Whoever fasts during Ramadan out of sincere faith and hoping to attain Allah's rewards, then all his past sins will be forgiven." (Bukhari)

So given this unparalleled opportunity, how can we best take advantage of it? Two often overlooked issues to keep in mind are:

Know why you're fasting:

Many people fast as a ritual, without truly understanding its meaning. Others reduce it to a simple exercise in empathy with the poor. While this is a beautiful consequence of fasting, it is not the main purpose defined by Allah. Allah says in the Qur'an: "Fasting is prescribed for you as it was prescribed for those before you, that you may attain taqwa (God-consciousness)." (Qur'an, 2:183) By controlling and restraining our physical needs, we gain strength for the greater battle: controlling and restraining our nafs (our soul's desire). When fasting, every hunger pang reminds us of God—the one for whom we have made this sacrifice. By constantly remembering Allah and sacrificing for Him, we are made more aware of His presence, and in that way we increase our taqwa (fear and consciousness of Him). The same thing that prevents us from the sin of sneaking in food while no one else is watching trains us to avoid other sins while no one else is watching. That is taqwa.

Don't make fasting just hunger and thirst:

The Prophet ﷺ has said, "Whoever does not give up forged speech and evil actions, Allah is not in need of his leaving his food and drink." (Al-Bukhari)

The Prophet ﷺ also warns us: "Many people who fast get nothing from their fast except hunger and thirst, and many people who pray at night get nothing from it except wakefulness." (Darimi) While fasting, understand the whole picture. Remember that fasting is not just about staying away from food. It is about striving to become a better person.

And in so striving, we are given a chance to escape the darkness of our own isolation from God. But like the sun that sets at the end of the day, so too will Ramadan come and go, leaving only its mark on our heart's sky.

WE BURIED A MAN TODAY: A REFLECTION ON DEATH

I wrote this in the car on my way back home from the burial of a righteous soul. May Allah subhanahu wa ta`ala (swt) *have mercy on him and his family. Ameen.*

We buried a man today. And here I am now on my way home in the caravan of the living. For now.

For now, you and I are in the caravan of the living. But not because we're headed for a separate land. Not because they're going and we are not. Only because our caravan lagged behind. Right now we're driving back to our homes, our beds, our TVs, our stereos, our jobs, our exams, our friends, our Facebook, and Gchat. Right now we're driving back to our distractions, our idols, our deceptive illusions. But that's just it. I'm not driving back to my home, my bed, my TV and my stereo. I'm not returning to my job, my exams, my friends, my Facebook and Gchat. I'm not on my way back to my distractions, illusions and idols. I'm driving back to where I began. I'm driving now to the very same place he went to. I'm on my way to the same place. I just don't know how long my drive will take.

I'm driving back to where I began: with God. Because God is *Al-Awal* (the Beginning) and God is *Al-Akhir* (the End).

My body is taking me there, but it's only a vehicle. When I get there, it will stay behind. As he did today. My body came from the ground and it will go back to the ground, as it came. It was only a shell, a container for my soul. A companion for a while. But I'll leave it here when I arrive. Arrive—not depart. Because that's my home. Not this. That's why when Allah (swt) is calling the back the righteous soul, He says, '*irjiee*': return. (Qur'an, 89:28)

The beautiful, noble soul that we buried didn't depart from life today. He just entered a higher—and God willing—better level of it. He only arrived home. But the body is made of the material world and so he had to leave it here. The body is of the lower world, the world where we need to eat and sleep and bleed and cry. And die. But the soul is of the higher world. The soul has only one need: to be with God.

And so while the body cries and bleeds and feels pain from the material world, the soul is untouched by these things. There is only one thing that can cut or stab or hurt the soul. There is only one thing that can kill it: depriving it of its only need: to be close to its Originator, to be near God. And so we should not weep for the arriving soul—It isn't dead. We should weep instead for the one whose body is alive, but whose soul is dead because of its alienation from that which gives it life: God.

And so the believing soul races home, even while in this life.

O Lord, make my soul a sanctuary, a fortress within. That no one and nothing can disturb. A place of calm, silence, and serenity, untouched by the outside world. The soul that Allah (swt) calls *al-nafs al mutmaina* (the reassured soul). (Qur'an 89:27) The soul that Allah (swt) calls back saying:

يا أيتها النفس المطمئنة

ارجعي إلى ربك راضية مرضية

فادخلي في عبادي

وادخلي جنتي

"(To the righteous soul will be said:) 'O (thou) soul, in (complete) rest and satisfaction! Come back thou to thy Lord—well pleased (thyself), and well-pleasing unto Him! Enter thou, then, among My devotees! Yea, enter thou My Heaven!'" (Qur'an, 89:27-30)

WHY AREN'T MY PRAYERS BEING ANSWERED?

Question: Why aren't my prayers being answered?

Answer: May Allah reward you for asking such an honest question, and may He guide us towards the truth. *Ameen.*

I think what happens in this type of situation is that we mix up **our means** and **our ends**. When we make *du'a'* for a good husband, for example, is that strong marriage a means or an end? I think many people take it as an end, which explains much of the disillusionment and disappointment that often follows (ironically in both cases: whether we get it or we don't). Like everything in this *dunya*, marriage is only a means—a means to reach Allah. So if we pray for it and we don't get it, perhaps Allah has chosen another means for us—perhaps through hardship, the purification it may cause and the *sabr* it builds, to bring us to that end: Allah. It may be, as only Allah knows best, that had He given us that amazing husband we made *du'a'* for, it would have made us heedless and therefore not achieve our end at all.

Instead of seeing it like this, however, I think the problem is, we are seeing things as just the opposite. The *dunya* (that great job, certain type of spouse, having a child, school, career, etc.) is our end and *Allah* is the means that we use to get there. We use that means, through making *du'a'*, to achieve our end (whatever it is that we're making *du'a'* for), and then get disappointed when our means (Allah) didn't come through for us. We throw our hands up in the air and say our *du'a'* are not being answered. Our means just isn't coming through for us!

But, Allah isn't a means. He is the end. The ultimate objective of even *du'a'* itself is to build our connection to Allah. Through *du'a'* we become closer to Him. So, I think the problem is that our focus is wrong. That's why I love the *du'a'* of *istikhara* so much. It's just perfect because it acknowledges that Allah only knows best, and then asks for Him to bring what is best and take away what is not best. The focus of that *du'a'* is not that which you are asking for. The focus is what is best in this life and next. This is not to say that we cannot make *du'a'* for things specifically that we want. On the contrary, Allah loves for us to ask of Him. But it means that once we ask, do our part to the utmost, and put our trust in Allah, we are pleased with what Allah chooses for us. And we realize that Allah answers all *du'a'* - but not always in the form we expect. And that is simply because our knowledge is limited, and His is unlimited. In His infinite knowledge He may send us what He knows to be better for us in achieving the ultimate end: the pleasure of Allah (swt).

Wa Allahu `alam (and Allah knows best).

FACEBOOK: THE HIDDEN DANGER

We live in an iWorld. Surrounded by iPhones, iPads, MYspace, YOUtube, the focus is clear: Me, my, I. One need not look far to see this obsession with the self. In order to sell, advertisers must appeal to the ego. For example, many ads appeal to the part of us that loves power and being in charge. DirectTV tells you: "Don't watch TV, direct TV!" Yogurtland says: "You rule! Welcome to the land of endless yogurt possibilities, where *you rule* the portions, the choices and the scene."

But advertisers aren't the only ones who appeal to our ego. There is a global phenomenon that provides a breeding ground and platform for that ego. And it's called Facebook. Now, I'll be the first to assert that Facebook can be a powerful tool for good. It is, like many other things, what you make of it. A knife can be used to cut food which feeds the hungry, or it can be used to kill someone. Facebook can be used for great good—after all it was Facebook that helped facilitate the toppling of a dictator. Facebook can be used as a powerful tool to organize, call, remind, and unite. Facebook can also be used to strengthen our connection to God and to each other… Or Facebook can be used to strengthen the hold of our *nafs* (lower self or ego).

The Facebook phenomenon is an interesting one. In each and every one of us is an ego. It is the part of ourselves that must be suppressed (if we are to avoid Anakin's fate of turning to the dark side, that is). The danger of feeding the ego is that, as the ego is fed, it becomes strong. When it becomes strong, it begins to rule us. Soon we are no longer slaves to God; we become slaves to ourselves.

The ego is the part of us that loves power. It is the part that loves to be seen, recognized, praised, and adored. Facebook provides a powerful platform for this. It provides a platform by which every word, picture, or thought I have can be seen, praised, and 'liked'. As a result, I begin to seek this. But then it doesn't just stay in the cyber world. I begin even to live my life with this visibility in mind. Suddenly, I live every experience, every photo, every thought, as if it's being watched, because in the back of my mind I'm thinking, "I'll put it on Facebook". This creates a very interesting state of being, almost a constant sense that I am living my life on display. I become ever conscious of being watched, because everything can be put up on Facebook for others to see and comment on.

More importantly, it creates a false sense of self-importance, where every insignificant move I make is of international importance. Soon I become the focus, the one on display. The message is: I am so important. My life is so important. Every move I make is so important. The result becomes an even stronger *me*-focused world, where I am at the center.

As it turns out, this result is diametrically opposed to the Reality of existence. The goal of this life is to realize the Truth of God's greatness and my own insignificance and need before Him. The goal is to take myself out of the center and put Him there instead. But Facebook perpetuates the illusion of the exact opposite. It strengthens my belief that because of my own importance, every inconsequential move or thought should be on display. Suddenly what I ate for breakfast or bought at the grocery store is news, important enough to publish. When I put up a picture, I wait for compliments; I wait for acknowledgement and recognition. With the number of likes or comments, physical beauty becomes something that can now be quantified. When I put up a post, I wait for it to be 'liked'. And I am ever conscience of—and even compete in—the number of "friends" I have. (Friends, here, is in quotation marks because no one knows 80% of their "friends" on Facebook.)

This preoccupation and rivalry to acquire more, is mentioned in the Quran. God says:

$$\text{أَلْهَاكُمُ التَّكَاثُرُ}$$

"The mutual rivalry for piling up (of worldly things) has preoccupied you." (Qur'an, 102:1)

Whether that rivalry is in piling up wealth, or friends and 'likes' on Facebook, the result is the same: We have become preoccupied by it.

Facebook also strengthens another dangerous focus: the focus on other people, what they're doing, what they like. *What they think of me.* Facebook feeds the preoccupation with others' assessment of me. Soon, I enter the orbit of the creation. Inside that orbit, my definitions, my pain, my happiness, my self-worth, my success and my failure is determined by the creation. When I live in that orbit, I rise and fall with the creation. When the people are happy with me, I'm up. When they're not, I fall. Where I stand is defined by people. I'm like a prisoner because I have given up the keys to my happiness, sadness, fulfillment, and disappointment to the people to hold.

Once I enter and live in the orbit of the creation—rather than the orbit of God—I begin to use that currency. See, the currency of God's orbit is: His pleasure or His displeasure, His reward or His punishment. But, the currency of the orbit of creation is: the praise and criticism of people. So, as I enter deeper and deeper into that orbit, I covet more and more of its currency, and I fear more and more of its loss. While I'm playing Monopoly, for example, I covet more and more of its currency. And it feels great to be 'rich' for a moment. But when the game is over, what can I buy in the Real world with Monopoly money?

The human currency of praise is Monopoly money. It feels great for a moment to collect, but when the game is over, it's worthless. In the Reality of this life and the next, it's worthless. And yet, I even covet this false currency in my worship. In this way, I fall victim to the hidden shirk: Riyaa (showing off in worship). Riyaa is a consequence of living in the orbit of the creation. The deeper and deeper I enter into that orbit, the more I become consumed with gaining human praise, approval and recognition. The more I enter that orbit, the more I fear loss—loss of face, loss of status, loss of praise, loss of approval.

Yet the more I fear the people, the more I become enslaved. True freedom only comes when I let go of the fear of anything and anyone other than God.

In a profound *hadith* (Prophetic teaching), a man came to the Prophet ﷺ and said: "O Messenger of God, direct me to an act, which if I do, God will love me and people will love me." He ﷺ said: "Detach yourself from the world, and God will love you. Detach yourself from what is with the people, and the people will love you." [Ibn Majah]

Ironically, the less we *chase after* the approval and love of the people, the more we gain it. The less needy we are of others, the more people are drawn to us and seek our company. This *hadith* teaches us a profound Truth. Only by breaking out of the orbit of the creation, can we succeed with both God and people.

So while Facebook is indeed a powerful tool, let it be a tool of your freedom—not a tool of your servitude to yourself and the assessment of others.

THIS IS AWAKENING

It's hard to describe the feeling. Imagine living your entire life in a cave and believing it was your whole world. Then suddenly you step outside. For the first time in your life, you see the sky. You see the trees and the birds and the sun. For the first time in your life, you realize that the world you once knew was false. For the first time, you discover a Truer, more beautiful Reality. Imagine the high of that realization. For a moment, you feel you can do anything. Suddenly, nothing from your previous life in the cave matters. You become empowered, fully awake, fully alive, fully aware for the very first time. It is an unexplainable feeling. This is the spiritual high that comes with newly discovered Truth.

This is Awakening.

A convert to Islam knows this feeling. A born Muslim who comes back to the deen knows this feeling. Any human being, who lives their life away from God, and returns, knows this feeling. This state is what Ibn ul Qayyim (RA) calls 'yaqatha' (awakening) in his book 'Madarij Al Salikeen' (Stations on the Path to God). He describes this state as the first station on the path to Allah. This is the state sometimes referred to as the "convert zeal". When a person first converts or starts coming back to Allah they are often full of motivation and energy that others do not have. The reason for this energy is the spiritual high, characteristic of this state.

Characteristics of the Station of Awakening:

Allah makes worship easier- While in this state, worship becomes much easier. A person is so driven and motivated that they may easily sacrifice everything for the sake of the new reality they have discovered. This zeal can take a person from 0 to 60 in no time. It's like being on spiritual steroids. The strength you have is not from your own self, but from an aid that was given to you. In this case the aid is given by God. Some may advise not changing too much, too fast. I don't think fast change is the problem. I think arrogance is. I think hopelessness is. If Allah gives you a gift whereby you are able to do more, use it. But thank Him—not yourself, for that ability. And know that the heightened state is temporary. You may go from 0 to 60 in a very short time due to it, but when the high passes, don't lose hope and let yourself slip back to 0.

Temporary- Like every state in this life, this state is temporary. Life is never linear. And neither is the path to God. Not realizing this can cause despair and hopelessness once it passes.

Pitfalls of This State:

The 2 pitfalls associated with this state correspond to not understanding the characteristics of the state listed above. These pitfalls are also the 2 causes of stagnation on the path to God: arrogance/complacency and hopelessness. The arrogant person already feels they are good enough, so they stop striving. The hopeless person believes that they will never be good enough, so they stop striving. Two opposite maladies, leading to the same result: To stop moving on the path to God.

Arrogance- The first pitfall corresponds to not understanding that the increased ability to worship came from God and is a characteristic of the state—not the individual! The one who doesn't understand this wrongfully attributes the heightened ability to worship to one's own righteousness. This false attribution is very dangerous because it leads to arrogance and self-righteousness. Rather than realizing this heightened 'religious state' is a gift from God, the worshiper feels a sense of hidden pride and may look down on others who don't share similar zeal.

Despair and Hopelessness- This pitfall corresponds to not understanding that like all states in life, the spiritual high is temporary. This does *not* mean you have failed nor done something wrong! Most people know what it feels like after the Ramadan high has passed. The instability of the 'high' is a characteristic of life. And that lesson is one even Abu Bakr (RA) had to learn.

One day Abu Bakr (RA) and Hanzala (RA) came to the Prophet ﷺ and said: "Hanzala is a hypocrite, Messenger of Allah! The Messenger of Allah, may Allah bless him and grant him peace, said, 'Why is that?' I said, 'Messenger of Allah, when we are with you, you remind us of the Garden and Fire and it is as if we could see them with our eyes. When we leave your presence, we attend to our wives, children and estates in a state of great heedlessness.' The Messenger of Allah, may Allah bless him and grant him peace, said, 'By the One in whose hand my soul is, if you were to remain in the state you are in when you are in my presence and in the *dhikr (remembrance)*, the angels would shake hands with you on your bed and in the street, but, Hanzala, different times are not the same.' three times." [Muslim]

After the Spiritual High Has Passed:

The most important part of this journey is never giving up! Know that you don't feel the same zeal, not because you have failed at something. The dip that follows the high is a natural part of the path! Just as the Prophet ﷺ explained to Abu Bakr (RA), these ups and downs are part of the path. And had we always remained in the high, we wouldn't be human. We'd be angels! The determining aspect for success is not so much what we do when we're up. The question is what we do when were down—when we're *not* feeling it. The key to succeeding on this path is that once you do reach your 'low', you keep going, knowing that it's normal.

Shaytan's Traps:

Remember Shaytan will get at you in different ways depending you your state.

When You're High- When you're high, he'll try to get you by making you arrogant. He'll try to get you by making you look down on others. He'll try to get you eventually by being so pleased with yourself that you don't think you need to keep striving because you are already so great (and better than others around you). He will consistently make you look at those who appear to do less than you, to justify your own shortcomings. For example, if you don't wear hijab, he'll make you think, "There are hijabis that do x, y, z bad things! At least I don't do those things! I do x, y, z good things that hijabis don't do!" Or if you slacken in prayer, you may think, "At least I'm not clubbing or drinking like so and so." Remember, Allah isn't grading on a curve. It makes no difference what others are doing. We all stand alone on the Day of Judgment. And this is just a tool of Shaytan to make us stop striving.

When You're Low- But when you're low, shaytan will try to get at you differently; he'll try to get you by making you hopeless. He'll try to make you believe that you're worthless and that there's no point in trying. He'll try to make you believe you are a failure and no matter what you do, you'll never get back to where you once were! Or he may try to make you believe that you're too 'bad' for Allah to forgive you. As a result, you may let yourself fall further. You may have been up once, and then felt so bad about yourself because you started to slacken in your worship. And maybe because of your previous self-righteousness you didn't give people permission to make mistakes or be weak. This ends up becoming self-destructive because it further translates to not giving yourself 'permission' to make mistakes and be weak.

Since you believe you don't have permission to be human and fallible, when you do make a mistake, you are so hard on yourself that you lose hope. So you let yourself go. You may end up committing more sins, which only makes your hopelessness worse! And it becomes a self-perpetuating vicious cycle. Shaytan will also try to make you believe that you shouldn't try to repent or pray because you'd be a hypocrite since you are such a 'bad' person. He wants you to despair in the mercy of Allah. That's what he wants! These are all lies, of course. But he's good at what he does, after all. When you have sinned, that's when you need to turn to Allah even more—not less!

To protect yourself from this downward spiral, remember that the lows are part of the path. Remember that 'futoor' (the dip) is part of being human. Once you realize that this does *not* mean you failed or that you are a hypocrite (like Abu Bakr (RA) thought), you can keep from giving up once you get there. The key is to develop certain habits which become your 'bare minimum'. That means no matter how you feel, how unmotivated, how low, you still do these things at the very least. You realize that when you're at your low, it's going to be harder, but you struggle to keep doing them. For example, the bare minimum is the 5 daily prayers at their appointed times. This should *never* be compromised no matter *how much* you're 'not feeling it'. They should be considered like breathing air. Imagine what would happen if every time you were exhausted or in a bad mood you decided not to breathe!

It is preferred to have other rituals that are part of the 'bare minimum'. For example, stick to certain extra prayers and athkar or daily Quran—even if it's little. Remember that Allah loves a small **consistent** action more than a huge inconsistent one. If you hold onto certain essentials during your 'low', you will ride the wave of iman and come back up, insha Allah. And, God willing, when you do go back up, you'll be at a higher place than your last 'high'.

Know that the path to Allah is not a flat one. Your iman (faith) will go up and down. Your ability to worship will go up and down. But know that for every dip, there is also a rise. Just stay patient, stay consistent, don't lose hope and seek help in Allah. The path is hard. The path will have bumps and drops. But, like all things in this life, this path will come to an end. And that end will make it all worth it!

Allah says:

يا أيها الإنسان إنك كادح إلى ربك كدحا فملاقيه

'Oh mankind, indeed you are ever toiling towards your lord, painfully toiling…But you shall meet Him' (Qur'an, <u>84:6</u>)

WOMEN'S STATUS

THE EMPOWERMENT OF WOMEN

When the companion of the Prophet ﷺ entered a town to bring them the message of Islam, he put it very beautifully. He said, "I have come to free you from the servitude of the slave and bring you to the servitude of the Lord of the slave."

Within this statement lies a powerful treasure. Locked within these words, is the key to empowerment and the only real path to liberation.

You see, the moment you or I allow anything, other than our Creator, to define our success, our failure, our happiness, or our worth, we have entered into a silent, but destructive form of slavery. That thing which defines myself-worth, my success and my failure is what controls me. And it becomes my Master.

The master who has defined a woman's worth, has taken many forms throughout time. One of the most prevalent standards made for woman, has been the standard of men. But what we so often forget is that God has honored the woman by giving her value in relation to Himself—not in relation to men. Yet, as western feminism erased God from the scene, there was no standard left—but men. As a result the western feminist was forced to find her value in relation to a man. And in so doing she had accepted a faulty assumption. She had accepted that man is the standard, and thus a woman can never be a full human being until she becomes just like a man: the standard.

When a man cut his hair short, she wanted to cut her hair short. When a man joined the army, she wanted to join the army. She wanted these things for no other reason than because the "standard" had them.

What she didn't recognize was that God dignifies both men and women in their distinctiveness–not in their sameness. When we accept men as the standard, suddenly anything uniquely feminine becomes by definition inferior. Being sensitive is an insult, becoming a full-time mother—a degradation. In the battle between stoic rationality (considered masculine) and selfless compassion (considered feminine), rationality reigned supreme.

As soon as we accepted that everything a man has and does is better, all that followed was just a knee-jerk reaction: if men have it—we want it too. If men pray in the front rows, we assume this is better, so we want to pray in the front rows too. If men lead prayer, we assume the imam is closer to God, so we want to lead prayer too. Somewhere along the line we'd accepted the notion that having a position of worldly leadership is some indication of one's position with God.

But a Muslim woman does not need to degrade herself in this way. She has God as the standard. She has God to give her value; she doesn't need a man to do this.

Given our privilege as women, we only degrade ourselves by trying to be something we're not–and in all honesty–don't want to be: a man. As women, we will never reach true liberation until we stop trying to mimic men, and value the beauty in our own God-given distinctiveness.

And yet, in society, there is another prevalent "master" which has defined for women their worth. And that is the so-called standard of beauty. Since the time we were little, we as women, have been taught a very clear message by society. And that message is: "Be thin. Be sexy. Be attractive. Or…be nothing."

So we were told to put on their make-up and wear their short skirts. Instructed to give our lives, our bodies, and our dignity for the cause of being pretty. We came to believe that no matter what we did, we were worthy only to the degree that we could please and be beautiful for men. So we spent our lives on the cover of Cosmo and we gave our bodies for advertisers to sell.

We were slaves, but they taught us we were free. We were their object, but they swore it was success. Because they taught you that the purpose of your life was to be on display, to attract and be beautiful for men. They had you believe that your body was created to market their cars.

But they lied.

Your body, your soul was created for something higher. Something so much higher.

God says in the Quran: "Verily, the most honored of you in the sight of God is the one who is most righteous." (Quran, 49:13)

So you are honored. But it is not by your relationship to men—either being them, or pleasing them. Your value as a woman is not measured by the size of your waist or the number of men who like you. Your worth as a human being is measured on a higher scale: a scale of righteousness and piety. And your purpose in life–despite what the fashion magazines say–is something more sublime than just looking good for men.

Our completion comes from God and our relationship with Him. And yet, from the time we were little, we, as women, have been taught that we will never reach completion until a man comes to complete us. Like Cinderella we were taught that we are helpless unless a prince comes to save us. Like Sleeping Beauty, we were told that our life doesn't fully begin, until Prince Charming kisses us. But here's the thing: no prince can complete you. And no knight can save you. Only God can.

Your prince is only a human being. God may send him to be your companion—but not your savior. The coolness of your eyes—not the air in your lungs. Your air is in God. Your salvation and completion are in His nearness—not the nearness to any created thing. Not the nearness to a prince, not the nearness to fashion or beauty or style.

And so I ask you to unlearn. I ask you to stand up and tell the world that you are a slave to nothing—not to fashion, not to beauty, not to men. You are a slave to God and God alone. I ask you to tell the world that you're not here to please men with your body; You're here to please God. So to those who mean well and wish to 'liberate' you, just smile and say: "Thanks, but no thanks."

Tell them you're not here to be on display. And your body is not for public consumption. Make sure the world knows that you will never be reduced to an object, or a pair of legs to sell shoes. You are a soul, a mind, a servant of God. And your worth is defined by the beauty of that soul, that heart, that moral character. So, you don't worship their beauty standards; you don't submit to their fashion sense. Your submission is to something higher.

Therefore, in answering the question of where and how a woman can find empowerment, I find myself led back to the statement of our Prophet's ﷺ companion. I find myself led back to the realization that true liberation and empowerment lies only in freeing oneself from all other masters, all other definitions. All other standards.

As Muslim women, we have been liberated from this silent bondage. We don't need society's standard of beauty or fashion, to define our worth. We don't need to become just like men to be honored, and we don't need to wait for a prince to save or complete us. Our worth, our honor, our salvation, and our completion lie not in the slave.

But, in the Lord of the slave.

A LETTER TO THE CULTURE THAT RAISED ME

Growing up, you read me the Ugly Duckling. And for years I believed that was me. For so long you taught me I was nothing more than a bad copy of the standard (men).

I couldn't run as fast or lift as much. I didn't make the same money and I cried too often. I grew up in a man's world where I didn't belong.

And when I couldn't be him, I wanted only to please him. I put on your make-up and wore your short skirts. I gave my life, my body, my dignity, for the cause of being pretty. I knew that no matter what I did, I was worthy only to the degree that I could please and be beautiful for my master. And so I spent my life on the cover of Cosmo and gave my body for you to sell.

I was a slave, but you taught me I was free. I was your object, but you swore it was success. You taught me that my purpose in life was to be on display, to attract, and be beautiful for men. You had me believe that my body was created to market your cars. And you raised me to think I was an ugly duckling. But you lied.

Islam tells me, I'm a swan. I'm different—it's meant to be that way. And my body, my soul, was created for something more.

God says in the Qur'an, "O mankind, indeed We have created you from male and female and made you peoples and tribes that you may know one another. Indeed, the most noble of you in the sight of Allah is the most righteous of you. Indeed, Allah is Knowing and Acquainted." (Qur'an, 49:13)

So I am honored, but it is not by my relationship to men. My value as a woman is not measured by the size of my waist or the number of men who like me. My worth as a human being is measured on a higher scale: a scale of righteousness and piety. And my purpose in life—despite what the fashion magazines say—is something more sublime than just looking good for men.

And so, God tells me to cover myself, to hide my beauty and to tell the world that I'm not here to please men with my body; I'm here to please God. God elevates the dignity of a woman's body by commanding that it be respected and covered, shown only to the deserving—only to the man I marry.

So to those who wish to 'liberate' me, I have only one thing to say: "Thanks, but no thanks."

I'm not here to be on display. And my body is not for public consumption. I will not be reduced to an object, or a pair of legs to sell shoes. I'm a soul, a mind, a servant of God. My worth is defined by the beauty of my soul, my heart, my moral character. So, I won't worship your beauty standards, and I don't submit to your fashion sense. My submission is to something higher.

With my veil I put my faith on display—rather than my beauty. My value as a human is defined by my relationship with God, not by my looks. I cover the irrelevant. And when you look at me, you don't see a body. You view me only for what I am: a servant of my Creator.

You see, as a Muslim woman, I've been liberated from a silent kind of bondage. I don't answer to the slaves of God on earth. I answer to their King.

A WOMAN'S REFLECTION ON LEADING PRAYER

On March 18, 2005, Amina Wadud led the first female-led jum'ah (Friday) prayer. On that day, women took a huge step towards being more like men. But did we come closer to actualizing our God-given liberation?

I don't think so.

What we so often forget is that God has honored the woman by giving her value in relation to God—not in relation to men. But as Western feminism erases God from the scene, there is no standard left—except men. As a result, the Western feminist is forced to find her value in relation to a man. And in so doing, she has accepted a faulty assumption. She has accepted that man is the standard, and thus a woman can never be a full human being until she becomes just like a man.

When a man cut his hair short, she wanted to cut her hair short. When a man joined the army, she wanted to join the army. She wanted these things for no other reason than because the "standard" had it.

What she didn't recognize was that God dignifies both men and women in their distinctiveness—not their sameness. And on March 18, Muslim women made the very same mistake.

For 1400 years there has been a consensus of the scholars that men are to lead prayer. As a Muslim woman, why does this matter? The one who leads prayer is not spiritually superior in any way. Something is not better just because a man does it. And leading prayer is not better, just because it's leading. Had it been the role of women or had it been more divine, why wouldn't the Prophet ﷺ have asked Ayesha or Khadija, or Fatima—the greatest women of all time—to lead? These women were promised heaven—and yet they never led prayer.

But now, for the first time in 1400 years, we look at a man leading prayer and we think, "That's not fair." We think so although God has given no special privilege to the one who leads. The imam is no higher in the eyes of God than the one who prays behind.

On the other hand, only a woman can be a mother. And God has given special privilege to a mother. The Prophet ﷺ taught us that heaven lies at the feet of mothers. But no matter what a man does he can never be a mother. So why is that not unfair?

When asked, "Who is most deserving of our kind treatment?" the Prophet ﷺ replied, "Your mother" three times before saying "your father" only once. Is that sexist? No matter what a man does he will never be able to have the status of a mother.

And yet, even when God honors us with something uniquely feminine, we are too busy trying to find our worth in reference to men to value it—or even notice. We, too, have accepted men as the standard; so anything uniquely feminine is, by definition, inferior. Being sensitive is an insult, becoming a mother—a degradation. In the battle between stoic rationality (considered masculine) and selfless compassion (considered feminine), rationality reigns supreme.

As soon as we accept that everything a man has and does is better, all that follows is a knee-jerk reaction: if men have it, we want it too. If men pray in the front rows, we assume this is better, so we want to pray in the front rows too. If men lead prayer, we assume the imam is closer to God, so we want to lead prayer too. Somewhere along the line we've accepted the notion that having a position of worldly leadership is some indication of one's position with God.

A Muslim woman does not need to degrade herself in this way. She has God as a standard. She has God to give her value; she doesn't need a man.

In fact, in our crusade to follow men, we as women never even stopped to examine the possibility that what we have is better for us. In some cases we even gave up what was higher only to be like men.

Fifty years ago, society told us that men were superior because they left the home to work in factories. We were mothers. And yet, we were told that it was women's liberation to abandon the raising of another human being in order to work on a machine. We accepted that working in a factory was superior to raising the foundation of society—just because a man did it.

Then, after working, we were expected to be superhuman—the perfect mother, the perfect wife, the perfect homemaker—and have the perfect career. And while there is nothing wrong, by definition, with a woman having a career, we soon came to realize what we had sacrificed by blindly mimicking men. We watched as our children became strangers and soon recognized the privilege we'd given up.

And so only now—given the choice—women in the West are choosing to stay home to raise their children. According to the United States Department of Agriculture, only 31 percent of mothers with babies, and 18 percent of mothers with two or more children, are working full-time. And of those working mothers, a survey conducted by Parenting Magazine in 2000, found that 93% of them say they would rather be at home with their kids, but are compelled to work due to 'financial obligations'. These 'obligations' are imposed on women by the gender sameness of the modern West, and removed from women by the gender distinctiveness of Islam.

It took women in the West almost a century of experimentation to realize a privilege given to Muslim women 1400 years ago.

Given my privilege as a woman, I only degrade myself by trying to be something I'm not—and in all honesty—don't want to be: a man. As women, we will never reach true liberation until we stop trying to mimic men, and value the beauty in our own God-given distinctiveness.

If given a choice between stoic justice and compassion, I choose compassion. And if given a choice between worldly leadership and heaven at my feet—I choose heaven.

MANHOOD AND THE FACADE OF BEING HARD

Last week my sister called. She has been studying abroad since summer began, so naturally I was thrilled to hear from her. After hearing how she was, I asked about her new home. With her living in a Muslim country, I felt assured that everything would be fine. For that reason, what she described next was a complete shock. She began to describe a place where a girl can hardly leave her house without being verbally harassed by men walking by. She said that the catcalling was no longer the exception; it had become the rule. Then she told me about a Muslim girl she knew. The girl was riding in a taxi and when she arrived at her stop, she handed the driver his money. In many of these countries there are no strict meters, and since the fare is somewhat arbitrary, the driver became angry. Eventually the altercation escalated to such a degree that the driver grabbed the girl by the shoulders and began to shake her. At this, the girl became angry and insulted the driver. The driver then punched the young woman in the face.

At this point, I was extremely disturbed. However it was what my sister said next that was most devastating. Nearby, there was a group of men who saw what was happening, and rushed to the scene. Naturally they came to help the girl.

No. They stood and watched.

It was at this point in the story that I began to wonder. Suddenly I found myself questioning every definition of masculinity I had ever believed in. I wondered how a man — not one, but many — can stand and watch a woman be abused, and do absolutely nothing about it. It made me question what ideals define what it means to be a man in today's society. Had the definition of masculinity become so distorted as to be reduced to just unbridled sex drive? Had the image of the 'knight in shining armor' really been replaced by visions of macho, catcalling boys in the street?

Most of all, it got me thinking about what it means to be a Muslim man today. I wondered if our dominate definitions as Muslims are really what they should be. Today, a man is expected to be stoic, unemotional, inexpressive, tough, and unbending. Physical aggression is glorified and emotional expressiveness ridiculed. I then decided to examine the epitome of what it means to be a man. I decided to look at the Prophet ﷺ.

One of the most common definitions of manhood today is the lack of emotional expressiveness. It is almost universally believed that to cry is 'unmanly' and weak. And yet the Prophet ﷺ described it very differently.

When the Prophet ﷺ was handed his daughter's son who was dying, his eyes flooded with tears. His companion Sa'd then told him, "What is this, Prophet of God?" He ﷺ said, "This is a mercy that the Almighty has made in the hearts of His servants. And surely God has mercy to the merciful ones among His servants." [Bukhari]

But today, a man is not only expected to hide feelings of sadness, he is taught early on that even other emotions are not to be expressed. During the time of the Prophet ﷺ, there were some men who believed the same. Once while a villager was present, Prophet Muhammad ﷺ kissed his grandsons on the forehead. At that, the villager said with surprise, "I have ten children. I have never kissed any of them!" Prophet Muhammad ﷺ looked at him and said, "He who does not have mercy will not have mercy upon him." [Bukhari] In fact, with regards to showing affection, the Prophet ﷺ was very clear. He said: "If a man loves his brother in faith, he should tell him that he loves him." [Abu Dawud]

The Prophet ﷺ used to also show a great deal of affection towards his wives. Aisha reported that the Prophet ﷺ would only enjoy his meals when she would sit next to him. They would drink from one cup and he would watch where Aisha would place her lips on the cup so that he could place his lips on the exact position. He would eat from a bone after she would eat from it, placing his mouth where she had eaten. [Muslim]

The Prophet ﷺ used to also help around the house, contrary to another widely held myth of masculinity. Aisha reported, "The Prophet Muhammad ﷺ used to stitch his clothes, milk the goats and help in the chores inside the house." [Bukhari & Muslim]

But, perhaps one of the most common myths of what a man should be is the idea that a man should be 'tough'. Gentleness is widely considered only a feminine trait. And yet the Prophet Muhammad ﷺ said: "Allah is gentle and loves gentleness. He gives for gentleness what He does not give for harshness, nor for anything else." [Muslim] In another hadith, he says, "He who is deprived of gentleness is deprived of good." [Muslim]

And yet so much of that gentleness has been lost from our modern definition of masculinity. It is frightening when a boy can consider it manly to sexually harass a woman on the street, but consider it no question of his manhood to stand and watch while a girl is being hit. It makes you wonder if maybe our image of what is 'manly' in fact resembles a Hollywood gangster more than it does our beloved Prophet ﷺ.

UMMAH

DROP THE PREFIX

What kind of Muslim are you? The question seems odd, but for those who seek to divide and conquer Islam, the answer has become increasingly important. Even more disturbing are the labels we assign ourselves.

In our families few of us can say we've never disagreed with our siblings. But when a family member makes a mistake—even a big one—or has a view we don't agree with, even fewer of us decide to divorce that family and change our name. Today, the same is not true of our Muslim family.

Today, we're no longer just 'Muslim'. We're 'progressives', 'Islamists', 'traditionalists', 'salafis', 'indigenous', and 'immigrants'. And each group has become so alienated from the other, that we've almost forgotten that we share a common creed.

While real differences do exist within our ummah, something very serious has gone wrong. Within the fold of Islam, differences are not only tolerated— they're encouraged as a mercy from God. But as soon as we label and marginalize any who disagree with us, our downfall begins. Once we accept and internalize these labels as our main source of identity, the result is disastrous. As a result, we create our own camps, attend only our own gatherings and conferences; soon enough, we're talking only to those who agree with us. Dialogue within the ummah disappears, our differences become only more polarized and our views become more extreme. Before long, we stop caring about what happens to the 'other' group of Muslims around the world, as we amputate limbs from the unified body our Prophet ﷺ taught us we were. The 'other' (who happen to still be our brothers) become so foreign—even despised—that we no longer wish to be referred by the same family name, and even join our enemies against them.

Suddenly those differences, that were once a mercy, become a curse–and a weapon to defeat Islam. Our enemies "summon one another to attack [us] as people, while eating, invite others to share their food." (Abu Dawud)

On March 18, 2004 RAND, the influential U.S. think tank, released a report to help 'civilize' Islam by effacing it and remaking it in the image of Western secularism. In the report, *Civil Democratic Islam: Partners, Resources, Strategies,* Cheryl Benard writes, "Modernism, not traditionalism, is what worked for the

West. This included the necessity to *depart from, modify, and selectively ignore* elements of the original religious doctrine."

In order to "depart from, modify, and selectively ignore" elements of Islam, Benard suggests a simple strategy: label, divide, control. After labeling each group of Muslims, she suggests pitting one group against each other. Among other strategies, Benard suggests "encourag[ing] disagreements between traditionalists and fundamentalists," and "discourag[ing] alliances between traditionalists and fundamentalists."

By succeeding at this division and supporting the 'Modernist'/ 'Progressive' Muslims, Bernard hopes to invent a 'civil democratic' Islam that is less backwards and problematic. More specifically, she hopes to create an Islam that will surrender itself to the hegemony of the Neo Conservative Agenda.

So if the first step to deforming Islam is to exploit the labels that exist, let's say: "Thanks, but no thanks." God tells us: "And hold firmly to the rope of Allah all together and do not become divided." (Qur'an, 3:103) So although we really appreciate this effort to 'civilize' us and our religion—we'll have to pass. You only reform something that's corrupt or outdated. And you only fix something that's broken.

And while it's nice of you to want to call us 'modern' or 'moderate,' we'll do without the redundancy. Islam is by definition moderate, so the more strictly we adhere to its *fundamentals*—the more *moderate* we'll be. And Islam is by nature timeless and universal, so if we're truly Islamic—we'll always be modern.

We're not 'Progressives'; we're not 'Conservatives'. We're not 'neo-Salafi'; we're not 'Islamists'. We're not 'Traditionalists'; we're not 'Wahabis'. We're not 'Immigrants' and we're not 'Indigenous'. Thanks, but we'll do without your prefix.

We're just Muslim.

BE MUSLIM, BUT ONLY IN MODERATION

In his first 2004 presidential debate, Senator John Kerry began the night in the favor-of-the-day. Answering his first question, Kerry explained that America needed to isolate the "radical Islamic Muslims":

> "I have a better plan to be able to fight the war on terror by ... beginning to isolate the radical Islamic Muslims, not have them isolate the United States of America."

At first, the statement sounded redundant-even uneducated. A Muslim is, by definition, a follower of Islam, and is therefore, by definition, "Islamic". Saying "Islamic Muslims" was a lot like saying, "American Americans".
So was Kerry just being repetitive? Or was his statement perhaps more telling that even he realized? Are all Muslims "Islamic"? Well, the truth is-no. Not the good ones, at least.

More and more the underlying assumption seems to be that Islam is the problem. If Islam, as a faith, is in essence radical, the less "Islamic" something is the better. And thus a 'moderate Muslim'--the much coveted title--is only moderately Muslim and therefore only moderately bad. Saying this would be like telling someone to only be 'moderately black' so as not to be too violent.
Conversely, a Muslim who is too "Islamic" is then by definition "radical" - a "radical Islamic Muslim" - and must be dealt with (isolated).

In fact, Mona Mayfield understood these rules well when she defended her husband - wrongfully accused of participating in the Spain bombing.

"We have a Bible in the house. He's not a fundamentalist -- he thought it was something different and very unique", Mayfield told the associated press of her husband's conversion to Islam.

To prove his innocence, Mayfield tried to downplay her husband's commitment to Islam. She even felt the need to justify his conversion-as if that were his crime.

Mosque administrator Shahriar Ahmed took a similar approach to defend Mayfield. "He was seen as a moderate," Ahmed told reporters. "Mayfield showed up for the Friday ritual of shedding his shoes, washing his bare feet and sitting on the carpets to hear services. He did not, as some devout Muslims do, pray five times a day at the mosque."

The implication here is that Brandon Mayfield's guilt or innocence was in some way related to how many times he prayed at the mosque. Ahmed even went on to assert, "He was on the less religious side if anything."

These 'less religious' icons of what an 'acceptable' Muslim should look like can be found all over the media. Irshad Manji, media entrepreneur and author of The Trouble with Islam, is one of the most celebrated of these icons. Manji is widely published and has appeared in all the top media outlets. She even received Oprah's Chutzpah Award for "gutsiness".

Although Manji refers to herself as a "Muslim refusenik", the media refers to her as the model of a "practicing Muslim". Daniel Pipes, a board member of the United States Institute of Peace, calls her a "courageous, moderate, modern Muslim". But interestingly, Manji's ideas have less to do with Islam than Pipes' ideas have to do with peace. A Washington Post article describes Manji's epiphany about prayer-the cornerstone of the Islamic faith:

> "Instead, she said, she began praying on her own. After washing her feet, arms and face, she would sit on a velvet rug and turn toward Mecca. Eventually, she stopped this as well, because she did not want to fall 'into mindless submission and habitual submissiveness'."

Manji is welcome to her opinion about this practice of 1.5 billion people worldwide. She is also welcome to abandon any and all of these practices. But Manji is not simply depicted as an insignificant woman who decided not to pray. Her personal decision to abandon central tenants of her faith-so long as that faith is Islam- is portrayed as a fight for freedom. A fight against tyranny. She is 'courageous' and 'gutsy', a model for other not-too-Islamic Muslims to follow.

Making this the model is like asking someone not to be 'too black' or 'too Jewish' as if these were in essence bad or violent and anyone who struggled only to be 'moderately black' or 'moderately Jewish' was a freedom fighter.
For example, Manji told the Washington Post: "The violence is going to happen, then why not risk it happening for the sake of freedom?"

Yes. Freedom is good. Manji may have said it better. Kerry may have said it subtler. But a business management professor at California's Imperial Valley College said it truer: "The only way to end Islamic terrorism is to eliminate the Islamic religion."

But regardless of how you say it, one thing is for sure: when it comes to Islam these days-less is definitely more.

UNSPEAKABLE TRAGEDY AND THE CONDITION OF OUR UMMAH

I think there's a place in the human mind where we hide when there's nowhere left to go. And perhaps there's a part of the human heart where we relive forever unthinkable tragedy. However, for the people in Syria and Palestine today, that tragedy is not just an image of the mind or heart; it is the only reality they know.

As I stand helplessly watching the carnage in these lands, I too find myself unsure of where to go. I look for a place inside my mind, a place where I can make sense of the senseless and imagine that it isn't really happening. I drift between sadness, anger, depression, and back, but in the end I return to one relentless question:

Why?

Why is this happening to us? Why are we suffering all over the world? Why are we so helpless to stop it? Why are we so politically powerless in the very country we are citizen to? Why do we scream at the top of our voices, writing letters and calling representatives in the White House, only to have them continue mantras like: "Israel has a right to defend itself?" Why are we at this point? Why?

We have to ask why.

We have to stop and really examine where we are as an *ummah* (nation) and what we have become. There was once a time when Muslims were revered in the world, a time when we were loved by our friends and feared by our enemies. Today we have become the most targeted, vilified, and hated group in the world. In a recent Gallup poll, more than half of Americans said their opinion of Islam is "not too favorable" or "not favorable at all", and 43 percent admit harboring at least "a little" prejudice against Muslims—more than double the percentage reported towards Christians, Jews or Buddhists.

However we are not just hated. In many places, we are being tortured, killed, and stripped of our belongings. Where we are not physically targeted, we are stripped of our rights, falsely accused, and even falsely imprisoned. In fact, the widespread hatred of Muslims has become so deep that anti-Muslim rhetoric has become the accepted bigotry of choice. It is so accepted that it is even used by some people to get ahead politically.

This situation that we as an *ummah* find ourselves in was described in detail more than 1400 years ago. The Prophet Muhammad ﷺ said to his companions (*radi Allahu `anhum*): "The people will soon summon one another to attack you as people, when eating, invite others to share their food." Someone asked, "Will that be because of our small numbers at that time?" He replied, "No. You will be numerous at that time: but you will be froth like that carried down by a torrent (of water), and Allah will take the fear of you from the hearts of your enemy and cast *al-wahn* into your hearts." Someone asked, "O Messenger of Allah, what is *al-wahn*?" He replied, "Love of this *dunya* and hatred of death." [An authentic hadith recorded by Abu Dawud and Ahmad]

Just as the Prophet ﷺ predicted, the people have indeed summoned one another to attack us just as someone invites others to share their food. In this hadith, the Prophet ﷺ also describes us as becoming like the froth on the water. If you watch waves flowing in the ocean, you'll see that the thin layer of froth on the top is completely weightless and with little substance; the slightest breeze can destroy it. It does not even have enough power to determine its own course. Instead, it goes wherever the water carries it.

This is our condition, as the Prophet ﷺ described it. We must, however, return to the question of why. The Prophet ﷺ gives a clear answer for this question. He explains that the hearts will be filled with *wahn*. When asked about this word's meaning, the Prophet ﷺ responded with a few words that hold a truth deep in meaning. He said it was "love of this *dunya* (world) and hatred of death." The Prophet ﷺ here is describing a people who have become so completely engrossed in this life that it has made them selfish, materialistic, short-sighted, and heedless of their meeting with Allah. He is describing a people who have become so worldly that they have lost their moral character.

It is within the realm of this moral character that the condition of any people will change—either from good to bad or from bad to good. Allah *subhanahu wa ta`ala* (exalted is He) tells us, "Indeed, Allah will not change the condition of a people until they change what is in themselves." (Qur'an, 13:11) It is, therefore, because of their character that the condition of a people can change from a world superpower to the froth on the ocean. And it is only by changing the hearts and character that what was once only froth on the ocean can once again become strong.

Hence, we as Muslims should never lose hope. The nasr (help and victory) for His deen is promised. The question is whether you and I will be part of it. Allah (swt) reminds us of this in the Qur'an when He says: "So do not weaken and do not grieve, and you will be superior if you are [true] believers." (Quran, 3:139)

It is only by our sincere faith and our striving, that Allah (swt) will ever change our condition. So for the sake of those bleeding in Syria and Palestine and all over the world today, we, as an *ummah*, need to wake up and return to Allah.

TODAY'S OPENING OF THE RED SEA: REFLECTIONS ON EGYPT

When Prophet Musa (as) stood in front of the Red Sea, a tyrant and his army approached from behind. Some of those in Musa's midst began to divide. Looking ahead, those people saw only defeat:

"And when the two bodies saw each other, the people of Moses said: 'We are sure to be overtaken.'"(Qur'an, 26:61)

But Musa (as) had different eyes. His eyes were spiritual eyes that saw through the illusions of worldly hardship and defeat. He saw through. With a heart connected to the Most High, looking at the same seemingly impossible situation, Musa saw only God:

قال كلا إن معي ربي سيهدين

"(Moses) said: 'By no means! My Lord is with me! He will guide me through!'" (Qur'an, 26:62)

And indeed Allah did just that:

"Then We told Moses by inspiration: 'Strike the sea with thy rod.' So it divided, and each separate part became like the huge, firm mass of a mountain. And We made the other party approach thither. We delivered Moses and all who were with him; But We drowned the others." (Qur'an, 26: 63-66)

Today in Egypt, we are standing in front of a Red Sea. Today in Egypt, a tyrant and his army are at our back. Today, there are some who see only defeat. However, there are others whose eyes are looking through the blockade to the path and the hope beyond it. Today in Egypt, there are some who—even with a tyrant at their back—are saying:

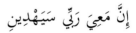

"Indeed my Lord is with me, He will guide me through."

One might wonder why, at such a critical time in history, we would retell an ancient story. Why would something that happened thousands of years ago be relevant today? The reason is that it is not just a story. Nor is it ancient. It is an everlasting sign and a lesson for all time. In the very next ayah, Allah says:

إن في ذلك لآية وما كان أكثرهم مؤمنين

"Verily in this is a Sign: but most of them do not believe." (Qur'an, 26:67)

It is a sign of the Reality of God and the secrets of this world. It is a sign that tyranny never wins and that obstacles are only illusions, created to test us, train us, and purify us. But most of all it is a sign of where success comes from. And it is a vision of what that success, against all odds—at a time we think we're trapped, defeated, and powerless—really looks like.

Some might ask why, if we are indeed on the side of God, does victory not come easily. Some might wonder why God doesn't just give the righteous victory without immense struggle and sacrifice. The answer to this question is also given by God. He tells us:

وما أرسلنا في قرية من نبيّ إلا أخذنا أهلها بالبأساء والضراء لعلهم يضرعون

"And We did not send a prophet in a town but We overtook its people with distress and affliction in order that they might humble themselves (reach a state of *tadaru'*)." (Qur'an, 7:94)

Here, Allah says that the purpose of the affliction is to reach a state of *tadaru*. *Tadaru* is humility before God—but it is not just humility. To understand the concept of *tadaru*, imagine yourself in the middle of an ocean. Imagine that you are all alone on a boat. Imagine that a huge storm comes and the waves become mountains surrounding you. Now imagine turning to God at *that* point and asking for His help. In what state of need, awe, dependency and utter humility would you be in? *That* is *tadaru*. Allah says that He *creates* conditions of hardship in order to grant us that gift. God does not need to make things hard for us. He creates those situations in order to allow us to reach a state of closeness to Him, which otherwise we'd be unlikely to reach.

That priceless state of humility, nearness and utter dependence on God is what the Egyptian people have been blessed with today. *Allahu akbar*—God is great. But Allah mentions another purpose for these hardships and struggles. He says:

وقطعناهم في الأرض أما منهم الصالحون ومنهم دون ذلك وبلوناهم بالحسنات والسيئات لعلهم يرجعون

"And We divided them throughout the earth into different groups. Of them some were righteous, and of them some were otherwise. And We tested them

with good [times] and bad that perhaps they would return [to obedience]."
(Qur'an, 7:168)

In Surat ali-Imran, Allah tells us:

"If a wound hath touched you, be sure a similar wound hath touched the
others. Such days (of varying fortunes) We give to men and men by turns: that
Allah may know those that believe, and that He may take to Himself from your
ranks Martyr-witnesses (to Truth). And Allah loveth not those that do wrong.
**Allah's object also is to purify those that are true in Faith and to
deprive of blessing Those that resist Faith.** Did ye think that ye would
enter Heaven without Allah testing those of you who fought hard (In His
Cause) and remained steadfast?" (Qur'an, 3:140-142)

Here, Allah describes the purpose of hardship as being *tamhees*. *Tamhees* is the
same word used to describe the heating and purifying of gold. Without heating
it up, gold is precious metal—but it's full of impurities. By performing
tamhees, a process of heating, the impurities are removed from gold. This is
what God also does with the believers. Through hardships, believers are
purified—just like gold.

And so too, are the Egyptians being purified. Only days before the uprising,
the world had considered the Egyptian youth a lost cause. We believed they
had lost their direction and their purpose. We believed that they had chosen to
live their lives on the streets, catcalling girls, or at internet cafes smoking
hookah. Through this hardship, the Egyptian youth have been brought back
from the dead.

Now, these youth are standing on the streets in defiance of tyranny, on their
knees praying, and with their hands facing the sky, calling on their Lord. The
same people who just days before barely prayed, stand today in front of
military tanks to bow down to their Creator. Only days before the uprising,
the tensions between Egyptian Muslims and Christians had grown to an all-
time high. Today the Christians and Muslims stand side by side in defense of
each other and their country. The same people who did not trust each other
the day before their 'heating', have come together as brothers and sisters, as
one body, to defend their streets, their homes, and their neighborhoods. And
through this hardship, a person who only days before lived for his cell phone,
sheesha, and cigarettes, has become willing to sacrifice his own life to give
freedom to his people.

Allah tells us in the Qur'an:

قل من يرزقكم من السماء والأرض أمن يملك السمع والأبصار ومن يخرج
الحي من الميت ويخرج الميت من الحي ومن يدبر الأمر فسيقولون الله فقل
أفلا تتقون

"Say: 'Who is it that sustains you (in life) from the sky and from the earth? Or who is it that has power over hearing and sight? And who is it that brings out the living from the dead and the dead from the living? And who is it that rules and regulates all affairs?' They will soon say, '(Allah)'. Say, 'Will you not then show piety (to Him)?'" (Qur'an, 10:31)

It is Allah who brings the living out of the dead. He has brought us back from the dead. Don't think for a moment that a single moment of this is not happening with a purpose—a deep, profound and beautiful, liberating purpose. For decades the Egyptian people have lived a life of fear. But when you let fear control you, you are a slave. Allah has liberated the Egyptian people from this slavery, by making them face–and overcome–their greatest fear. Allah has liberated the Egyptian people by allowing them to look their oppressor in the eye and tell him, and the whole world, that they will no longer live in fear. And so whether Mubarak stays or goes, lives or dies—it doesn't really matter. The Egyptian people have already been liberated.

They have been liberated.

Hosni Mubarak is irrelevant. He is nothing but a tool—a tool by which God carries out His plan for the Egyptian people and for the entire Ummah. A tool to carry out His plan to purify, beatify and liberate the Egyptian people and the Ummah. And whether we are in Egypt today or not is unimportant. Egypt is just one limb of our body. The purification of Egypt is a purification of the whole body of our Ummah. It is the purification of you and me. It is our chance to ask ourselves to what are we attached. What are we afraid of? What are *we* striving for? What do *we* stand for? And where are we going?

When a body is in a deep, deep slumber—a coma—it is only out of His infinite mercy that He sends us a wakeup call. It is only from His infinite mercy that He sends to us life where there was once only death. We were heedless, so He sent us a sign. We were asleep, so he woke us up. We worshiped this life, and preferred our material possessions to the liberation of a soul attached to, and afraid of nothing but Him—so He freed us.

How many people will experience something like this in their lifetime? How many people will experience the opening of a Sea, the humbling of a tyrant? Shouldn't we ask ourselves why *we* were chosen to see it? Shouldn't we ask ourselves what *we* were intended to learn, change, transform? Because if we think for a moment this is all just about the people of Egypt, then we have desperately missed the point. We were asleep, and Allah chose to wake us.

We were dead and Allah wants to give us life.

We were conditioned to believe that our enemy was outside of ourselves. That he had power over us. This is also an illusion. The enemy is inside of us. All external enemies are only manifestations of our own diseases. And so if we want to conquer those enemies, we must first conquer the enemy inside ourselves. This is why the Qur'an tells us:

$$له معقبات من بين يديه ومن خلفه يحفظونه من أمر الله إن الله لا يغير ما$$

$$بقوم حتى يغيروا ما بأنفسهم وإذا أراد الله بقوم سوءا فلا مرد له وما لهم من$$

$$دونه من وال$$

"Indeed, Allah will not change the condition of a people until they first change what is in themselves." (Qur'an, 13:11)

We must first conquer greed, selfishness, *shirk*, ultimate fear, love, hope and dependence on anything other than Allah. We must conquer *hubbad-dunya* (love of dunya)—the root of all our diseases, and all our oppression. Before we can defeat the Pharaohs in our lives, we must defeat the Pharaoh inside ourselves. So the fight in Egypt is a fight for liberation. Yes. But liberation from what? Who is truly oppressed? Are you and I free? What is true oppression? Ibn Taymiyyah *(ra) answers this question when he says:* "The one who is (truly) imprisoned is the one whose heart is imprisoned from Allah and the captivated one is the one whose desires have enslaved him." (Ibn al-Qayyim, *al-Wabil*)

When you are free inside, you will never allow anyone to take away your freedom. And when you have inner freedom, you can look through tyrants and thugs to the Lord of the tyrants and thugs. When you are free inside, you become unenslaveable, because you can only enslave a person with attachments. You can only threaten a person who is afraid of loss. You only have power over someone when they need or want something that you have the ability to take away. But there is only one thing which no person has the power to take away from you: God.

And so when we fight to free Egypt, on a grander and realer scale it is a fight to also free ourselves. It is a fight to free ourselves of the tyranny of our own *nafs* and desires. A fight to free ourselves from our own false attachments and dependencies, from all that controls us, from all that we worship—other than Him. It is a fight to free us from our own slavery. Whether we are slaves to the American dollar, to our own desires, to status, to wealth, or to fear—the purification of Egypt is a purification of us all.

That is why the formula for true success given to us in the Qur'an consists of two elements: *Sabr* (patience, perseverance) and *Taqwa* (fear of God alone):

يا أيها الذين آمنوا اصبروا وصابروا ورابطوا واتقوا الله لعلكم تفلحون

"O you who have believed, persevere and endure and remain stationed and fear God (alone) that you may be successful." (Qur'an, 3:200)

So if we watch Egypt today as if it is only a spectacle happening outside of ourselves, without cleaning, examining, and really changing ourselves and our lives, then we have missed its purpose.

After all, it isn't every day that a sea is opened before our very eyes.

POETRY

A LETTER TO YOU

It's hard to explain the freedom. It's so deep and so real. Looking through the confusion, the empty boxes and hollow images, I saw you—Dunya. You place veil after veil over my eyes. Trying to win me, deceive me, enslave me to your lies.

When the truth is you couldn't give me even a drop of water when I stood at your door begging. I was on my knees before you, desperate for you to fill me.

What I see now is a glimpse of clarity that only the stab of perpetual disappointment could carve. And I sit here surrounded by your henchmen, your army of liars sent to keep me in chains. But I won't be your prisoner anymore. I will no longer be that little girl lying awake at night thinking of you. I am no longer that heartbroken child wasting her tears on you. My unrequited love can no longer break me. You won't break me. I won't bend to your glitter and false promises. I am no longer that faithful subject standing before your false throne. My tears are no longer yours to have. And my heart is no longer your sanctuary.

You can't live here anymore.

I've traveled a long way to come here. Sometimes there were deserts where all I needed was a single drop of water that you couldn't give. Sometimes storms, where all I needed was a flicker of light to guide my path. And I asked you again and again for what you could not give. For all you have is pomp, boasting and chattel of deception. And so I found myself again and again in deserts without water, in darkness without light. But I am no longer your slave, for there was a man who came to liberate me from this. A man who came to liberate me from this slavery to the slave, and bring me to the slavery of the Lord of the slave.

I GRIEVE

I lifted my head

Once more

Only to see

The sun had set,

The trees had slept,

And they'd all gone home

I grieve.

The sky that was clear

is now covered with fog.

My path, I no longer see.

Why try…when it's all so gray?

I grieve.

Today I grieve

For what's been lost.

My forgotten people,

still on their knees

before a snow god in spring

I grieve.

They've forgotten that prayer

And to whom they should call.

The Essence replaced

by mundane ritual,

empty symbols.

Their hearts… so tired,

jaded and worn

I grieve.

We are a people

defeated…but not conquered.

And somehow

I feel my blood return.

I will stand.

I will try.

And from beyond my grief,

I will see…

There are a people you can't enslave.

A loyalty…you can't buy.

For a land may be occupied…

but never a soul.

From beyond my tears

I'll understand…

Today my people weep.

But tomorrow…Death will die,

as their tears give birth to a land

where…"on them shall be no fear

nor shall they grieve". (Qur'an, 2:262)

JUST MY THOUGHTS

There's a strange sadness today. It's not the kind that leaves you empty or lonely, or even wanting. It's the still kind, the kind that comes from a certain level of understanding, even acceptance.

I looked at this photo today, and every time I did, I found tears fill my eyes. It was a sunset on the beach. Stunning. And above it the ayah: *Rabanna ma khalaqta hatha batilan subhanak* (our Lord you have not created all of this for nothing, subhanak.)

And that's just it. All of this. The sadness, the accidents, the smiles, the peace, the pain, the love, the loss, and the sacrifice: it's not for nothing. It is not without purpose. It's not a mistake, some sort of oversight or a random course of events.

I looked at the image and suddenly I was filled with such a deep sense of nostalgia. For a time, I have no memory of.

وإذ أخذ ربك من بني آدم من ظهورهم ذريتهم وأشهدهم على أنفسهم

ألست بربكم قالوا بلى شهدنا أن تقولوا يوم القيامة إنا كنا عن هذا غافلين

"And [mention] when your Lord took from the children of Adam—from their loins—their descendants and made them testify of themselves, [saying to them], "Am I not your Lord?" They said, "Yes, we have testified." [This]—lest you should say on the day of Resurrection, "Indeed, we were of this unaware."" (Qur'an, 7:172)

I was overcome with the feeling of missing someone. Missing Him. Missing being with Him. Missing a time that was or will be. A time so certain, it is as if it already happened. That's why when Allah talks about the hereafter in the Quran, He uses the past tense.

When you fall in love with a work of art, you'd die to meet the artist. I am a student of the galleries of Pacific sunsets, full moon rises on the ocean, the clouds from an airplane, autumn forests in Raleigh, and first fallen snows.

And I'm dying to meet the artist.

"Some faces, that Day, will be radiant, looking at their Lord." (Qur'an, 75:22-23)

A REFLECTION ON LOVE

All of this love. Every piece. Every part of all the love in this world. The love they make poems with. The love of spellbinding novels. The love in songs. The love they tried to capture in a movie. The love of a mother for her child, of a child for her father. The love that liberates. The love that enslaves. The love you win. The love you lose. The love you chase. The love you live for. The love you know you'd die for. The love that makes men bleed. The love that swords have killed for. The love of fairytales and tragedy.

It is all just a reflection.

An echo. Of one single Source. Of a single love that you know, and I know, because we knew it before we could know. We were loved before we could love. You were given before you could give or know what it was to give. It is the love that your heart was created to know. It is the love that creates and sustains all love. It is the love that was before——and will remain after all else has passed away.

It is the love that was before…and will remain after all echoes have passed away.

I PRAYED FOR PEACE TODAY

I found myself praying for peace today.

I've been in and out of my mind a thousand times

I know You heard me.

I know I wasn't alone in that room,

shaking with the fear of fear,

the harrowing loneliness.

I cried out to You on my hands. On my knees.

With my face pushed down against the ground.

If I could have gotten lower, I swear I would.

Because that is helplessness, the truest kind…

The kind that knows nothing, not one leaf, or tear, or smile can be
without Him.

I learned something today.

Again.

This is dunya. Dunya. Not a place of ease. Only glitter.

The place where you have to feel cold and hungry.

The place where you have to worry and feel scared.

The place where it gets cold.

So cold, sometimes.

The place where you have to leave the people you love.

Where you can't get attached, because even if you do, it doesn't make it stay,
it just makes it hurt when it doesn't.

The place where happiness and sadness are only players, waiting for their next
line in a play…

Competing for their place on stage.

The place where gravity makes you fall and frailty makes you bleed.

The place where sadness exists, because it must.

And tears fall to remind you of a place where they don't.

Where they just don't.

And isn't that just it? Isn't jennah that place after all?

That place that Allah describes over and over and over in 2 ways?:

وَلَا خَوْفٌ عَلَيْهِمْ وَلَا هُمْ يَحْزَنُونَ

On them shall be no fear…nor shall they grieve.

But I'm still here, aren't I?

The scar on my flesh reminds me of that.

The burn on my arm left a scar that I love.

I love it because it reminds me how weak I am.

How human.

That I burn. That I bleed. That I break. That I scar.

Yes. It is here that I am. Here that I fall. Here that I cry.

Here, just the same, that You filled that room, and lifted me to humbleness, and an acute knowledge of my own powerlessness and excruciating need for You.

And then you took care of it.

Of course You did.

Of course.

Like Younus, and Musa, and his mother. You took care of it.

You are the Peace of the peaceful.

The Strength of the strong.

The lighthouse of Truth in this storm of lies.

So, I found myself praying for peace today.

ON THE STRUGGLE OF LIFE

I thought of You today

I thought of You and remembered those words You told me

In the most perfect way

You calmed my beating heart

And eased my breath

You told me those words and I carry them still

They lift me, fill me, undo the wear

Because more than pain, I am worn

I feel like I've lived this story for a thousand years

And I'm ready now to sleep

I'm ready to let go

I'm ready for the story to end now

I'm ready to feel your peace

And the sound of your voice

Telling me I'm done, I've won, I'm there

But I know I know this place

I've been here before

I'm going to sleep now

I'm going to sleep

Please don't ask

Please don't ask

Just let me sleep

Just let me sleep with your words upon my tongue:

'Oh mankind, indeed you are ever toiling towards your lord, painfully toiling…

But you shall meet Him' (Qur'an, 84:6)

STILLNESS

The sun is so beautiful in the early morning. It does something to the trees that you don't see any other time of the day. I think we all want the same thing: A quiet peace. Maybe just even a single moment of it, to close our eyes and just be okay.

For even a single second, to not feel worried about something, sad about something. To not crave something we don't—or can't—have. Just to be there, okay. Still. Silent. On the inside. Maybe that's what's so beautiful about this time of the day: The stillness.

And the hope that maybe this day will be different.

DIE BEFORE YOUR DEATH

Tell me I can get lost

Tell me I can lose myself in your Presence

In the overwhelming moment of real submission

Tell me I can remain forever broken

In You

For You

With You.

Tell me I can remain here forever

Away, while still here.

Did not the Prophet ﷺ say: "Die before your death"?

At first I thought maybe it was only a reminder

to remember our meeting with You.

But then I thought how I wish I could die before my death:

Have a soul that is no longer in this life—even while the body must remain.

A heart that is freed from the shackles of dunya—even while the legs must walk its streets.

Have a nafs that is in complete rest and satisfaction with its' Lord–even while the crumbling shell remains.

A soul that is already there—even before it is there.

A soul detached.

A nafs mutmainah—in the truest and deepest and realest sense (Quran 89:27)

For as the great scholar said, rahimahu Allah, "He who does not enter the paradise of this life, will not enter the paradise of the next."

SAVE ME

I have nothing but your generosity to put my hope in- Nothing. For I stand at Your door holding broken scraps…and yet you open. Save me from this storm. I am the most helpless of all your slaves. And I'm lost, wandering in the middle of a forest trying to find my way. But all the trees look the same, and each path just leads back to the beginning. No one finds their way out of this forest—except whom You save. Save me- For truly, truly I cannot save myself.

My Heart is an Open Book

My heart is an open book,
Torn open by my story.
Tell them you learned the lesson.
You'll learn it every time,
You seek completion in the incomplete.

You sought refuge in a straw house.
Then when the storm came,
You were bare and alone.
Exposed.
You spent years swallowing...
But it was only air.
And you wondered why it left you empty.

They told you stories
And you believed them...
Then waited for the tooth fairy
To bring you change.

And yet still you'd give anything
To make the story real.
Let it go.
There's a better story.
That isn't a story.
It's Real.
But in it the hero never dies

Or bleeds or cries.

Find the Real version.

Memorize it.

Write it on your heart.

And then,

Give it to the world to read.

Your heart is an open book.

THE STAB

Don't grieve at the stab.

It's only meant to free you.

From the chains that bind you to the earth

and shackle you to the shadows of people.

The mirage of water cannot quench.

But is so beautiful to the thirsty.

I'm afraid. Of never knowing another life.

Different. So different.

If I let go, will You take me higher?

Above grief, want, loss.

Above all that I've ever known.

Take me higher. Unbind me from the earth.

Like a vaccine, it sickens, to make you stronger.

The stab is temporary. The freedom, eternal.

NICHE

My bones want to melt
My muscles want to let go
My body wants to stop
Walking,
Struggling,
Fighting,
for air,
for life.
My mind painted a picture for me,
But now it's all in black and white.
The trees are bent, tired, closed.
My heart, the same
But still, my thoughts keep talking,
Walking,
Struggling,
Fighting,
For air,
For life.
How can you erase a picture so clear?
So real?
Tell me how to erase myself from it,
And lay my own tired steps to rest.
I see
I'm stumbling,
Not walking.
I'm tripping now
Not talking.
There's a pain inside my chest
Born of silence, grief, unrest
Who's there but me to claim it?

Who knows but me to name it?
I'm sorry for my apathy,
My lassitude at dawn.
I'm circling now through forests
Trying to find my niche.
Has inspiration come to me?
Whose voice is it I hear?
My own is sharp and deafening.
Who else could know my name?
It is only through His kindness
That the heart can speak
When the mind and body
are numb,
Only dragging.
Please come,
If only to quiet my thoughts.
I'm circling forests
On wings
Still searching for my niche.
I'm no longer
Walking,
Struggling,
Fighting.
I've won the air
I've won my life.

KEEP WALKING

Every day I get closer to our Meeting.
I feel like I've been walking this path for a thousand years
towards You…
and yet I'm still not there.
So close, and yet so far still

But I keep walking,
despite the tears,
despite the wind,
despite the skinned knees and broken bones,
despite the bruises and scars that make this heart what it is today,
I keep walking…
toward You.
There's only one direction,
one direction:
towards You.
From You, to You.
I have nothing else.
Nothing.
That is my poverty.

I keep walking
because behind every sun's setting is a rising,
behind every storm is a Refuge,
behind every fall is a rise,
behind every tear is a cleansing of the eyes.
And in every spot you've ever been stabbed, is a healing,
and the creation of skin stronger than it was.

I keep walking
because wallahi I have nothing but Your mercy.
I have nothing but Your promise
Your words
Your promise
that:

يا أيها الإنسان إنك كادح إلى ربك كدحا فملاقيه

O mankind, indeed you are laboring toward your Lord with [great] exertion and will meet it. (Qur'an, 84:6)

CPSIA information can be obtained at www.ICGtesting.com
Printed in the USA
BVOW001313140413

318068BV00007B/101/P

9 780985 751203